"Plantes and Finfrock brilliantly capture the essence of how to systematically ensure that a firm can effectively compete by creating differential advantage. Step-by-step they show how to integrate strategy, product, people, and processes for success, and how leadership and commitment at the top has to drive the initiative. This book is a must-read for all thoughtful executives and managers who want to break out of the mold of me-too competition."

—Greg W. Marshall, PhD
Charles Harwood Professor of Marketing and Strategy
Rollins College, Crummer Graduate School of Business

Beyond Price provides a holistic perspective on the vital strategic decisions facing leadership teams and best practices for their execution. The authors' easy-to-embrace framework will help you create a highly effective senior leadership team and fully engaged associates, advantages necessary in today's highly competitive B2B and consumer markets."

—Ron Zabel
Retired CEO, Springs Window Fashions

Beyond Price is a must read strategy and execution book for leaders who want to reposition their business for higher profitability and growth."

—Michael Ainsley
Former president and CEO, Sotheby's

"My company has secured a terrific market position in a highly competitive industry by following the authors' advice for differentiating your company. We are growing rapidly despite the presence of all the national competitors in our market. As important, business is fun again, helping us attract top-notch talent."

—Jay Loewi
CEO, The QTI Group

"At last, a 'how to' book on business strategy that is eminently readable and applicable to all. Few books get at fundamental strategy decisions, much less articulate them as clearly and meaningfully as the action-oriented 'things to consider and then do' provided by Plantes and Finfrock. It is a testimony to their method that the book manifests what they preach: differentiated from other business advice books; forward thinking yet steeped in business reality; providing exceptional value to the user."

—Marsha Lindsay, CEO of Lindsay Stone & Briggs and LSB
Brandworks University

"Differentiating a professional services firm is very challenging because our credentials are very comparable. *Beyond Price*, therefore, is a welcomed and highly pertinent guide to building a professional services firm clients and targeted prospects see as uniquely better than other qualified firms."

—William J. Bula, AIA, president and CEO, Flad & Associates

Beyond PRICE

Differentiate Your Company
in Ways That Really Matter

MARY KAY PLANTES
ROBERT D. FINFROCK

GREENLEAF
BOOK GROUP PRESS

Published by Greenleaf Book Group Press LLC
4425 S. Mo Pac Expwy, Suite 600
Longhorn Building, 3rd Floor

Austin, TX 78735

Distributed by Greenleaf Book Group LLC

For ordering information or special discounts for bulk purchases, please contact Greenleaf
Book Group LLC at 4425 S. Mo Pac Expwy., Suite 600, Austin, TX 78735, (512) 891-6100.

Design and composition by Greenleaf Book Group LLC
Cover design by Greenleaf Book Group LLC

Publisher's Cataloging in Publication Data
(Prepared by The Donohue Group, Inc.)
Plantes, Mary Kay.
   Beyond price : differentiate your company in ways that really matter / Mary
Kay Plantes, Robert D. Finfrock.
   p. ; cm.

   Content: Pt. 1: Know where you are -- Pt. 2: Design the business you want to
run -- Pt. 3: Create and manage your new business.

   ISBN: 978-1-929774-73-9

1. Product management--United States. 2. Marketing--Management. 3 Business--
Management. 4. Relationship marketing. I. Finfrock, Robert D. II. Title.

HF5415.15 .P52 2009
658.8   2008931123

Part of the Tree Neutral™ program that offsets the number of trees consumed
in printing this book by taking proactive steps such as planting trees in direct
proportion to the number of trees used. www.treeneutral.com

Printed in the United States of America on acid-free paper

08 09 10 11 12 13 14   10 9 8 7 6 5 4 3 2 1

First Edition

TreeNeutral

*For all leaders who aspire to better serve
coworkers, customers, investors, and communities
by building a thriving business.*

Contents

Foreword

In today's global economy, leaders face an arduous challenge meeting their revenue and profit growth targets. Relentless competition and increasingly powerful and informed customers are to blame. *Beyond Price* gives leaders an unusually pragmatic and thorough approach to winning without competition.

Becoming a unique company—separating your company and its product and services from the herds in ways that competitors cannot easily copy—is challenging. Many books, my own included, describe the characteristics of companies that have accomplished this and the overarching strategies behind their success. The books motivate leaders to try to copy the example companies' changes. Few if any books provide as convincing, accessible, and comprehensive a methodology for how to proceed as *Beyond Price*.

Beyond Price translates high-level and often hard-to-accept or difficult-to-execute ideas into a form that not only is readily understandable to readers but also quickly begins to sound like commonsense revelations, the "Why didn't I think of that?" The disciplined process that coauthors Plantes and Finfrock provide will help companies of all types become and remain "categories of one" in their markets. Leaders, especially those who've embarked on significant change in their organizations, will welcome the authors' savvy advice on how to deal with a recalcitrant leadership team.

Once you read *Beyond Price*, you'll be motivated and able to take your company to a higher level of performance.

—**JOE CALLOWAY**, speaker, consultant, and author of *Becoming a Category of One* and *Indispensable*, both John Wiley & Sons publications

Acknowledgments

A book is a journey, fueled by a deep purpose to educate and a willingness to learn, take risks, and be ruthlessly honest with one's limitations. This book started when Robert took over his father's struggling business as a young man out of college and Mary Kay left a prestigious university faculty position because her work lacked, for her, any deeper meaning. Along the way, our journeys intersected thanks to Robert's industry association, and we have both benefited enormously and grown as leaders and teachers.

Our sincere thanks go to Sue Reynard, who helped us make sure our writing was as logical as the framework we wanted to teach, and Pete Roether, who enhanced our descriptions. The team at Greenleaf Book Group has been terrific, from our initial dinner to the book's arrival on bookstore shelves. Robert's Finfrock Design-Manufacture-Construct coworkers, Glenn Valenta and Gail Kroll, gave up considerable work time to make sure *Beyond Price* makes sense to everyday business leaders. Nick Ecos, Dan Oestrich, Barry Callen, and Bill Steinburg, provided helpful insights at different stages of this book's writing.

Mary Kay's consulting business started the day her daughter Lauren was born. This book is being published as Lauren leaves for college. She compelled Mary Kay to model what composing the life and business you want to lead looks like. Friends that Mary Kay loves and family members she is forever indebted to know who they are. Thank you. And final thanks to Mary Kay's many clients and audiences across North America, whose courage in leading change and lessons in leadership helped shape this book.

Robert thanks Mary Kay for her role in the incredible transformation of his business and fulfillment of a long-term dream. He will leave an exciting and strong business to his sons. Robert is also thankful to his coworkers who were so willing to take the risk to win beyond price. Together, they have created a business model no one thought was possible. Finally, special thanks to the wonderful woman at Robert's side all along, his wife, Ginny.

—MARY KAY PLANTES and ROBERT FINFROCK

May 2008

Preface

Forget product innovation as a surefire solution to breaking free of price-driven competition. Even new-to-market products, services, and categories are rapidly dragged into price comparison battles as competitors copy what they see working well in a market.

Commoditization is the gravity of our marketplace, an economic force pulling competing products and services down to the same level, until price determines which company wins and which loses customers. This force is getting stronger each year as technology makes it easier and easier to copy competitors' product and service innovations, at the same time that globalization and the Internet are creating more copycat competitors. Furthermore, the Internet creates more powerful customers capable of searching out lower prices and creating auctions in which the lowest-priced bidder wins the order.

We cannot eliminate commoditization any more than we can eliminate gravity. All it takes is but *one* other similar offering and an experienced purchasing agent or knowledgeable consumer to make price all that matters in the competitive battlefield for market share. Not even product customization provides an escape.

The good news is that you can escape commoditization by strategically differentiating your entire business to create an enterprise that is hard for competitors to replicate. In doing so, you add unique customer benefits or customer cost savings across your entire offering, even in your most mature and price-sensitive markets.

Beyond Price will teach you how to innovate your business model to escape the gravity of commoditization. (Your business model carves out where your organization will compete and how it will win and retain customers. As such, it defines both your competitive strategy and growth strategy.) *Beyond Price* provides a disciplined approach that your leadership team can adopt to steer your business out of and away from commodity markets or to prevent falling into them in the first place.

Beyond Price is a welcome complement to other strategy books. Books and articles about blue oceans,[1] creating monopolies,[2] categories of one,[3] and innovation[4] provide terrific examples of differentiation but often leave readers wondering, "Now what do I do?" or, "Why are my company's differentiation efforts falling short of outcomes I expected?"

These questions remain unaddressed because the narrow focus of business strategy books leads the reader to think that a new strategy or innovation alone, if executed, will create needed change. Nothing could be further from the truth. *Beyond Price* identifies and integrates all the areas of change, beyond strategy and innovation, that a leadership team must address to break out of and stay out of commodity competition. It also describes how to translate these changes to the front line. *Beyond Price* addresses changes in

- Leadership beliefs and practices
- Market understanding process
- Business model strategy
- Sales and marketing planning
- Operational planning and process improvement and redesign
- Execution
- Culture

These topics have become separate writings in the business literature. As a result, focused books fill different sections of bookstores' business reading shelves, just as most business schools teach these topics in separate courses. No wonder leadership teams are left with the questions, "Where do we start, and how do we excel in our efforts to escape price-driven competition through differentiation?" *Beyond Price* captures in one integrated, easy-to-digest book those enduring economic principles and business practices you'd best not forget if you want your company to earn above-market returns and customer loyalty.

As such, the eight steps of *Beyond Price* create a framework that will help you understand your strategic leadership role and perform it in a way that leads to marketplace victories and financial success for your company. Adopting this framework as the leadership team's strategic agenda is at the heart of leaders building a company (and offerings) that are highly valued by target markets and never seen as "about the same" as the alternatives. In addition, each chapter will help you anticipate and overcome potential resistance as you lead the charge to create a unique company that delights your customers.

We wrote *Beyond Price* for a broad audience of leaders who want to take their company to the next level. Leaders of a small to midsize company, or a Fortune 1000 business unit or division, selling locally or globally all face growing price competition. We also hope that executives who have settled into business-as-usual because they have concluded, "Differentiating my company is a wasteful investment because customer decisions will always be about price," will read our book with an open mind.

Whether your company serves other businesses or consumers, you will find our book an easy-to-understand yet systematic guide to transform your company from a just-another-face-in-the-crowd, price-driven organization to a one-of-a-kind company whose offerings competitors will find hard to copy and whom customers will be delighted to discover. *Beyond Price* will give your leadership team a well-defined road map and route to build a genuinely thriving business.

BASED ON EXPERIENCE

The framework presented in *Beyond Price* works. Economist and coauthor Mary Kay Plantes has developed and successfully tested the process in a variety of companies of different sizes, participating in a broad array of business-to-business and consumer goods industries over the last twenty-two years. Coauthor Robert Finfrock has used it to transform his own company. You'll find stories from these and other companies sprinkled throughout the book, demonstrating that it is possible to become a highly differentiated competitor in any industry.

Introduction

Despite a highly educated and uniquely talented technical staff, Finfrock Industries won and lost business on price. A respected firm in its industry, Finfrock Industries was a midsize provider of precast/prestressed structural concrete components used in the construction of parking garages and other commercial buildings. The precast industry had turned into a commodity quagmire as the technology matured. General contractors (the purchasers of the precast components) based their purchasing decisions on cost and delivery alone. Financial returns were adequate at best, but there was a lot of red ink during economic downturns.

The company owner, coauthor Robert Finfrock, was then the chairman of his industry's national association. This role made him aware that what was happening to his business was far from unique.

Robert came to realize that all precast solutions, from the general contractors' perspective, had matured to the point where there was not much difference between competitors' offerings or, for that matter, between precast and competitive structural building materials. Buying on price and schedule was a sensible decision on customers' part. In short, from the purchaser's viewpoint, Finfrock Industries was just *one of many* qualified competitors with identical outcomes for the building project.

Robert had an intuition, although he could not quite explain why, that the only way to build a thriving business again was to move up the food chain, so to speak—to somehow deal directly with the building owners. They were the people with the most vested interests in the quality of Finfrock Industries' products and its ability to help owners save money and reduce risk during construction.

Robert tried to articulate his intuition about owners to other leaders in his company. Steeped in the "rules" of the construction market, they were hesitant to rock the boat and join Robert in a major change effort.

In hindsight, Robert's insight was a pivot point, because it led Robert and his management team to explore new directions. What would it take to successfully act on this new insight?

About that time, Robert met coauthor Mary Kay Plantes, a consultant who specializes in helping leadership teams innovate their firms' business models—to rethink what their business is all about—in order to grow more rapidly. She helped him understand the economic principles that created and controlled commodity markets and provided a road map for transforming a business to escape from those constraints. That was exactly what Finfrock Industries needed. Robert and his management team came to see that trying to get better at what they currently did would leave them in the same rut and get them nowhere. In fact, they realized that the rules driving the industry were flawed. They needed to start doing business differently—not just to redefine their offerings but also to reinvent the entire business that created their building project solutions.

Their next step was to define the company's unique and true strengths, around which Robert and his leadership team could build a new business model. They realized they knew more about how to cost-effectively design, manufacture, and erect parking garages and other building structures than any of the architectural-engineering firms and general contractors in the marketplace. Yet all too often, Finfrock Industries' sales and engineering professionals gave this knowledge away free of charge, in an attempt to get architects and contractors to favor Finfrock Industries with the "last look at price" during a request for proposal, bid, or auction process. The realization reinforced the need for doing business in a new way by selling directly to owners, because owners were the people who would gain the most value from the company's superior knowledge.

It became clear to the leadership team that the predominant way that general contractors, engineers, architects, and subcontractors like Finfrock Industries did business—with each separate company performing in its own self-interest—did not create the optimum solution for the building owner. What was most compelling about Robert's idea of selling to owners was that there was no company that offered a vertically integrated, truly turnkey precast building solution for parking garages and other structures. Being the first to do so would make Finfrock *a unique and more valued alternative for owners and developers.* The company could begin offering unique benefits—create a monopoly, in essence—rather than continue to suffer as *one of many* in a commodity bidding process. By being the single source of responsibility and self-performing much of the project, Finfrock Industries could create the highest-value solution for owners of parking garages and other structures—solutions that would maximize usable space and minimize cost and completion date risks for the dollars spent.

The vision that emerged was to turn what was a pure custom-engineered components manufacturing firm into a design-build construction firm. The change was not without its challenges: Finfrock Industries would have to learn how to handle everything from working with the customers to define their needs and wants related to a new building, to preparing architectural plans and specifications, to designing and making the precast parts, to completing construction of a building.

Robert recalls that the implications of that decision were scary: His company would have to develop expertise in a wide range of new skills. How quickly could they develop that knowledge and integrate it into the company? What if the change in strategic direction didn't work? Would his company lose the general contractor customers it currently had once it directly competed with them for owners' business?

The next two years were hectic, a blend of excitement and frustration mixed with high energy and long hours. The leadership team knew the general direction the company needed to go in, but it had a lot of work to do to define and develop into exactly what the company needed to look like to reach its vision of selling directly to owners. All that work happened through a detailed strategic thinking and action-planning process built on principles you'll find in this book.

Part of the initial work also included reshaping the management team itself. Although some original members quickly and easily accepted the new vision, others disagreed. Robert couldn't blame the dissenters who opposed the admittedly radical and risky changes. But he saw "business as usual" as being even riskier. He felt he needed people on the team who all interpreted the writing on the wall the same way, so that leadership could present a unified vision to the rest of the company.

In concert with completing the strategic plan, the company also started intensive education efforts. For example, Finfrock Industries had very limited experience working with other subcontractors such as electricians and plumbers. To educate the workforce, the company held hundreds of in-house seminars those first two years, and it continues workshop learning to this day. It also created a number of positions that were new to the company, such as architects and project managers. Selling to owners in these early years was limited to parking decks, where general contracting skills were more straightforward than were office and other types of commercial buildings.

At the end of about two years, the company could confidently call itself Finfrock Design-Manufacture-Construct, Inc. (Finfrock D-M-C)[5], which is what it has been ever since. The company then had the major pieces in place and moved into other commercial construction markets such as offices, mixed-use structures (e.g., retail and residential), and multifamily housing (e.g., college dormitories).

What was initially seen as a huge risk for the company has turned into a huge boon. Since implementing the new strategy, Robert's business has increased more than tenfold, with much higher profit margins and total dollar profits exceeding former sales levels. Previous general contractor customers, impressed by Finfrock D-M-C's capabilities, now hire the company to construct entire buildings within sizable commercial developments.

Though in theory Finfrock's design-manufacture-construct offering could also become commoditized, Robert thinks the likelihood of that happening any time soon or in a way that threatens the survival of Finfrock D-M-C is remote at best. Why? Because his company continues to build advantages that will be hard for others to copy. Anybody can compete based on a product, but Finfrock D-M-C has a complete system, skill set, and culture that are very hard to duplicate. Robert and his team continue to apply the principles in this book to remain a category of one.

Building a Strategically Differentiated Business Model

What Robert's company ended up doing was to define a strategically differentiated business model: a new vision for how and where the company would compete. A *business model* describes where a business competes—its target market(s) and offerings; its *value proposition*—why customers will choose it over other alternatives; and why competitors won't be able to easily or affordably copy its value proposition.

A strategically differentiated business model, executed effectively, will provide your organization with the following:

- Customers willing to pay a premium for your offering
- Longer-term relationships with customers and suppliers
- Different parts of the organization working collaboratively because they have a shared understanding of where and how you want to win business
- Easier and faster decision making related to pursuing opportunities
- Easier resolution of conflicts that naturally arise among different parts of the organization
- Better resource leveraging because the company is far more focused

The rest of this book will walk you through the steps needed to make the kind of significant changes that Robert's company made so you need not compete primarily on price and lose price premiums for innovations. You'll end up with a truly differentiated business whose offerings will be hard for competitors to copy.

Although our book is set up as a series of three parts divided into steps, achieving the kind of transformations described in this book is an evolutionary cycle: Decisions are made and acted on, then revisited and further enhanced when more and better information is available. You may work on more than

---

CAN YOU SKIP STEPS?

We suspect that most readers will be best off starting from Step 1 and working straight through to Step 8—at least the first time they try to apply the concepts and methods we discuss. However, you can really start with any chapter, depending on where you think your company needs the most change. For example, if you have strategically differentiated your business model and you think you have a market-understanding process that is as strong as your financial-understanding process, then you could pick up at Step 5 to build a stronger company.

PART I: **Know Where You Are**

Step 1: Understand the root cause of your problem. What is it that's trapping you in a commodity market? The economic forces can't be changed, only your response to them.

Step 2: Forget customer driven; become market driven. If you focus only on the stated needs of your current customers, it's unlikely your business will ever break out of the commodity trap. You need to take a broader look at the market. Becoming market driven in the strategic assessment of your business will let you drive the market by creating new-to-market categories and offerings.

Step 3: Conduct a strategic assessment. Become a consultant to your own business. Scour the marketplace for useful market insights that will help you redefine your biggest opportunities and risks. Ask a different set of questions about your business, questions that will shed new light on strategic risks and opportunities and point the way to business model innovations within your reach.

PART II: **Design the Business You Want to Run**

Step 4: Design a new strategically differentiated business model. There's no purpose in going through this effort if all you do is jump from one commodity market to another. The purpose of this step is to help you synthesize the information and strategic insights you've gathered in the assessment to define a new business model that will confer strategic differentiation. You'll have a unique selling proposition that your target market can't turn down and evidence you'll deliver on it. The new business model will likely broaden or narrow your target markets and redefine what business you're in.

Step 5: Realign the leadership team. Your leadership team consists of the key managers who have to steer your ship in a new direction. It is essential that each member understands that his or her role is first and foremost to run his or her areas of responsibility on behalf of the senior team. If each leader continues to maximize the success of his or her part of the organization, irrespective of other parts or strategy execution, your differentiation efforts will fail.

Step 6: Create a meaningful corporate aspiration. Once the leadership team is aligned, you can roll out the new business model to the rest of the management team or workforce. With them, you then define or refine the company's vision, purpose, and guiding principles. How this is done will determine whether you will build commitment to the new direction or let resistance and resentment stop your change efforts.

PART III: Create and Manage Your New Business

Step 7: Establish strategic goals and create an annual planning process to achieve them. The new vision and strategically differentiated business model will become a reality only if the company defines exactly what it will take to get there and builds the needed changes into its management structures and plans.

Step 8: Align culture with strategy. If the changes you arrive at are anywhere near as big as those faced by Finfrock D-M-C—and odds are they will be if you're serious about breaking out of commodity markets—you will end up redefining your business and how it operates. This step will show you how to modify your culture to better support the new business model. You will fall short of reaching your strategic goals and vision without culture alignment.

one step at one time. The eight-step *Beyond Price* process will be your guide (see pages 6 and 7). It will help you conceptualize and lead an ongoing change process that otherwise feels and often becomes so chaotic that both leaders and employees alike lose their motivation to keep going.

As Robert Finfrock's story has illustrated, going through these steps takes a lot of time and effort. But he'll testify that it's all worth it. Before, he and his management team were living in a constant fire drill, focused on solving problems and operational issues while cutting costs. Now they get to hear customers say they are elated with what the company has done for them. These customers are enthusiastic advocates for Finfrock D-M-C. And that's how any company knows it has a thriving future.

As it Appears

Many leaders think their business is on a fairly
calm river . . .

As it Will Be

They do not realize that all businesses are headed
into commodity markets. The time to change is
before it's too hard to turn around.

PART I
Know Where You Are

If you do not turn around, you just might end up where you are headed!

A major change in strategy must be based on a deep understanding of what's happening with your business and your market. The first three steps of the *Beyond Price* process help you uncover insights that can lead to new directions for your business.

Step 1: Understand the root cause of your problem.

Step 2: Forget customer driven; become market driven.

Step 3: Conduct a strategic assessment.

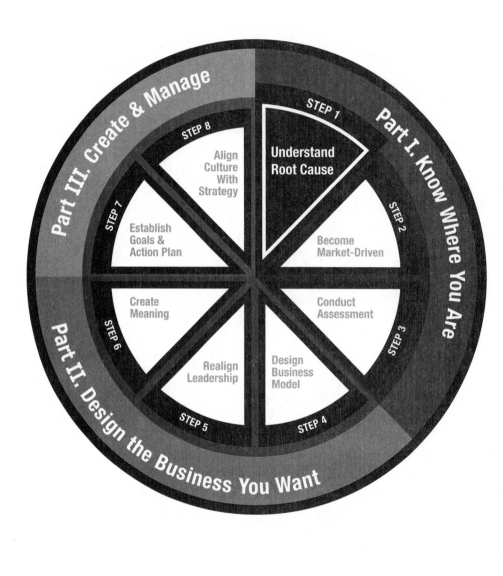

Step 1

Understand the Root Cause of Your Problem

Doing everything right is not always the right thing to do.

"How did this happen? How did I get to be a price-driven *survivalist*? I did everything right—improved the quality of my product, raised service levels, and listened to my customers. I even developed solid relationships with them and invested in the new products and services that they wanted! Where were the warning signs? Should I have seen it coming?"

These are the reactions of business leaders who are operating in *survival mode*, a market nightmare where the only thing that differentiates you from your competitors is price—or at least that is what your customers think. In survival mode, you think and act in ways that prevent you from circumventing competitors. Whether your company is a start-up or old-line, offers a service or is a manufacturer, sells to consumers or other businesses, sells direct or using other channels, there is a typical path to competing on price that makes frustration increasingly universal. It goes something like this:

You were the first company to offer a product, a quality level, a technology, a location, or a cheaper way of doing something. Your sales grew steadily and you used growing profits to improve your offerings, your quality, and your efficiency. Slowly, however, "me-too" offerings started to show up in the market. The quality and service levels that once differentiated your company's offerings suddenly were no longer enough. It became increasingly difficult or expensive to stand out in a crowded space or to attract the interest of purchasing agents or consumers. Other established businesses may have entered your market space with a breadth of offering advantages you could not match. Perhaps garage start-ups or overseas competitors entered the market with prices too low for your higher overhead as a larger, more complex business. Or, small and nimble niche companies entered with innovative products. When you finally closed the gap, what once differentiated your company and its offerings had become a customer expectation. Whatever the route, you found yourself mired in competition in which price increasingly determined who won or lost market share.

The fact is that most companies slip into competing primarily on price without even realizing it. There is no sudden shift in the wind, no bolt from the blue, no scurrying of small woodland creatures fleeing the impending cataclysm. It happens quietly and without notice while companies are working hard to do everything right—improving quality, reducing cost, adding beneficial features, introducing new products and line extensions, and speeding production.

Identifying When Commodity Markets Emerge

Commodity markets (also known as price-driven markets) shift power from sellers to customers, a shift that can happen under many different conditions. If any of these drivers sound familiar, you're likely competing in a commodity market or one that will become that shortly:

- It is easy for competitors to copy each other's technology and features.
- Markets are mature—that is, there have been no changes in products or services or their applications for an extended period of time. The products or services are solving the same problems today as they did in the past.
- A few customers make up a large percentage of your total revenue.
- Customers only want a standard product with no genuine customization.

- Customers pay low or no switching costs when changing to new suppliers.
- Customers can self-manufacture your product offering or self-perform your service.
- A particular supplier's products or services are not essential to the quality of the customer's finished goods or service.
- There are a number of acceptable suppliers that customers can consider.
- Customers' profit or income is low and being squeezed.

Buying power is demonstrated in the following types of statements:

- "I'll only accept qualified bidders—those that have the capabilities to provide this quality level within this time frame."
- "Tell me your final price."
- "Our auction is in three days."
- "Here's exactly what I want—read the request for proposal (RFP)."
- "The store brand is more than good enough for me."
- "Which item on the shelf has a coupon or is on sale this week?"

In fact, whether selling consumer products through retailers or selling business products to other businesses, any type of statement or gamesmanship by

---

YOU ARE HERE

Expected outcome: The leadership team will understand the marketplace dynamics that create a survival mode mentality and the role of strategic differentiation in defining a new beyond-price future.

Who is involved: The awareness of commodity market dynamics and its implications starts in the leadership but must eventually be a core understanding across the management team, if not the company as a whole.

Why this step is important: Leaders can get so involved in day-to-day operations that they accept commodity competition as a given, not something their company helped to create and can escape. A necessary condition of transformation is a leadership team that feels completely accountable for performance.

a customer whose primary motive is to lower prices by pitting one supplier against another is evidence of buyer power and commodity markets. Consumers participate in the same type of process by using search engines that point to best price offerings and sellers, or by relying more and more on coupons and sales events or promotions for brand decisions.

Sound familiar? Welcome to the twenty-first-century economy! But even though the prevalence of price-driven markets makes business success harder to come by, the underlying principles that create them have not changed since Adam Smith described economic markets. Revisiting these key principles can prepare you to escape from where you are today and avoid the slippery slope dragging you toward commodity competition.

Making Economics 101 Pertinent

Let's begin by taking another look at Economics 101. Remember that heavy book you had to carry around that read more like a math text? You probably wondered how economic theories would ever become pertinent to your love of engineering or management or advertising or whatever you really wanted to do for a living. We promise this chapter will be easier than your Economics 101 class and will definitely deliver more tangible results.

COLLEGE BOREDOM

COMPANY GOING PUBLIC THANKS TO ECON 101 WISDOM

HOWEVER YOU REACH YOUR CUSTOMER, VALUE RULES

Sales Representative   Store   Internet

We'll look at three basic economic principles from a more relevant perspective than that provided by your college economics professor. These principles explain why a strategically differentiated business model is necessary for healthy profitability. These economic principles do not lie to you. They are among the fundamental laws of the marketplace that create price-driven competition. They are the root cause of your business ending up in survival mode. *All of your strategic business decisions must be evaluated against these principles.*

ECONOMIC PRINCIPLE 1:
All purchase decisions are based on value, even in commodity markets.

Whether a specialty retailer is purchasing a luxury Rolex watch, whether a manufacturer is buying a critical component, whether a company or a consumer is buying a simple staple like paper towels, or whether a couple is purchasing a retirement-celebration cruise, the final purchase decision is *always* based on value. Even in price-driven markets, value rules. In business-to-business (or B2B) markets, the customer asks, "What will the offering do for my business and career success?" In consumer markets, "How am I or my family better off?" is the question. More specifically:

$$\text{VALUE} = \frac{\text{benefits the customer perceives}}{\text{the product or service delivers}} - \frac{\text{the total cost to}}{\text{customer to acquire}} \atop \text{those benefits}$$

Benefits are both primary and secondary.

- Primary benefits are tangible, easily perceived and evaluated or measured, and therefore easily compared to those of your competitors.
- Secondary benefits are intangible, and therefore hard to measure (such as emotional responses), yet also influence the comparison of suppliers.

Primary versus Secondary Benefits. An example: A primary benefit of a consumer or a delivery service purchasing a new hybrid car would be fuel cost savings. A secondary benefit of purchasing a hybrid car would be feeling proud about reducing the environmental impact of driving.

Costs are both direct and indirect.

- Direct costs are the dollar outlay—the purchase price you are charged.
- Indirect costs are additional costs you incur by purchasing one company's offering.

Direct versus Indirect Costs. An example: Switching banks to get a free checking account results in a low direct cost (just the cost of printing new checks), but it may cost you several hours to change any automatic transactions tied to your accounts and could result in a bounced check or two, which would be significant indirect costs.

How customers perceive the balance of real and emotional benefits that matter to them and costs to acquire them will determine whether they treat you as the unique provider of the highest value offering or just one of many providers of a commodity. Think about the products, companies, or services your business deals with in everyday life. To what suppliers are you most loyal as a customer? (It may be possible that you think of them more as strategic partners than as suppliers.) As a consumer, which products do you buy specifically by brand, and which do you buy solely on price? The difference reflects the cost/ benefit calculation that goes on endlessly in all business and personal purchasing decisions.

What does it mean when price determines which company or product a customer selects? It means that the customer considers the primary and secondary benefits of each competing alternative, net of their indirect costs, as essentially identical. Therefore, the purchase price (direct cost) is all that makes one supplier more or less attractive in terms of perceived value.

When purchase price becomes the sole difference in perceived value, your product or service has become a commodity. Facing this type of competition on a daily basis keeps your business stuck in survival mode.

It doesn't take much: Commodity competition can emerge with as few as two qualified, competitive offerings that meet customers' basic requirements. This is the reason why commodity markets emerge so often. In a capitalist system, every market is on a steady march toward commodity-like conditions that economists call *pure competition*. The march is shorter and shorter in recent years due to advances in technology and globalization, among other reasons. You can't escape commoditization pressures until you acknowledge they are there. Only then can you build a strategically differentiated business model that takes your company away from essentially equivalent competition and moves it into a market where you are the superior supplier or the only supplier.

IT'S THE BENEFITS THAT MATTER

When communicating with potential customers, companies too often focus on the attributes or features of their offering rather than its benefits. When selling to another business, for example, increasing your customers' revenue, lowering their costs, reducing their risk, improving their competitive position, lowering their investment, or increasing their productivity is a benefit. When you talk benefits, customers listen, whereas when you talk attributes such as quality or unique features first, the potential customer can say, "I have enough of that," or, "That doesn't matter to me." The door to a sale is then shut.

ECONOMIC PRINCIPLE 2: *The profit margin that a business earns depends on supply relative to demand.*

You have to know the rate-of-return principle like the back of your hand. Even in price-driven commodity markets, when too much demand is chasing too little supply, price escalates. The reverse is true, as well. Just look at the price of a

---

"IMPROVING" TO STAY EVEN

Economic Principle 2 also helps explain why the real winners of process improvements over the last decade have been customers, not suppliers. Your customer derives all the extra value you have created through process improvement, as long as at least one other company matches your quality or productivity improvement and is willing to offer the product or service at the same price you are charging or a lower price. That's right, *all* the quality and efficiency gains go to the customer, and you have done *nothing* to improve your margin or your market share. You remain in commodity quicksand.

Why? How can this be? You improve quality and lower costs and get *no* benefit to your bottom line?

That's right. When customers see you and the copycat competitor(s) as equivalent, they are able to extract the "best price" from you and your competitors. Such competition drives prices down to the old price plus the cost of any improvements. If better quality or improved productivity reduced costs, price competition among price-driven competitors drives prices down to the new lower cost. This is a phenomenon that is happening across the world in industry after industry.

Net-net, you have worked harder and made lots of improvements just to stay in business, thanks to the laws of supply and demand.

The impact of competition on price is why a primary role of purchasing in any organization—be it a retailer, a distributor, or a manufacturing company—is to get all suppliers to compete on the same terms. Purchaser communications, RFPs, and reverse auctions are different strategies to level the benefit and indirect cost field so that price is the significant variable differentiating suppliers. Because companies are forced to offer essentially the same thing, buyers are able to extract the lowest possible net price. Only the customer wins here.

snowblower in June, as compared to the same product in December. Individual companies have little control over these external factors.

ECONOMIC PRINCIPLE 3: *There is only one winner in a commodity market—the company with the lowest-cost structure.*

The only company to secure attractive returns in a commodity market is the lowest-cost supplier. These returns can be used to further lower costs, add new benefits, or do other things like dropping prices to increase market share. The only ongoing exceptions to this case are natural or government-granted monopolies or oligopolies, in which entry barriers are so steep that only a few companies serve the market and keep financial returns high through indirect price signaling. Periods of excess demand and limited supply are also exceptions, as excess demand is a tide that causes all boats to rise. But when the water returns to normal levels, the lowest-cost supplier in a price-driven market is the only company to earn attractive returns. Some companies, lacking the lowest-cost structure, may still remain in the market, making little or no return. But how much fun is this? And what could their future possibly hold? How will this type of company ever attract and retain talented employees to replace valued retiring employees?

The discussion of these three principles introduces a corollary pertinent to your strategic thinking. When companies in an industry choose different strategic target markets or different value propositions, more than one company in the industry can walk away with above-average returns. Neither is a commodity in this case.

> **Corollary:** *If companies divide the market, more than one winner can emerge.* Strategic differentiation is what divides the market for an industry's offerings. Still, you must remain unique to avoid commoditization of your offerings.

Implication: Determining the Need for Strategic Differentiation

If you cannot become the lowest-cost supplier in a market that is forcing you to compete primarily on price, there is only one way to earn consistently attractive returns. *You must become the only or clearly superior company to offer benefits that are highly valued by customers.* The process for lifting your company's offerings out of commodity market quicksand is called *strategic differentiation. Its end result is a strategically differentiated business model.*

In its simplest definition, *differentiation* means doing things differently from anyone else. Most often, companies think about differentiation of an individual product, service, or category. Strategic differentiation focuses on creating higher value across all your company's offerings in existing categories and creating new-to-market categories. It is not about differentiating one product line in your company or one of your brands. For a quick illustration of how this works, consider a sports team that has been successful over many seasons. When you look at how it operates, you can see how it differentiates itself from the competition.

WHY STRATEGIC DIFFERENTIATION
CREATES HIGHER PROFITS

Strategic differentiation addresses each of the three economic principles.

Principle 1: *Value.* You're focused on providing superior value that other businesses cannot duplicate across all your offerings. This includes existing offerings and new-to-market categories that emerge from your new business model.

Principle 2: *Supply versus demand.* You are avoiding the issue of excess supply pressures on price because you're offering differentiated benefits and overall value that your competitors cannot match. As long as the additional value you offer customers exceeds your cost to deliver this value, your returns will increase with strategic differentiation. There are two reasons for this:

- The higher value increases market demand for your product or service.
- The greater the difference between your business and the alternatives, the higher the customer sets the bar for other companies and brands to even be considered. The fewer qualified alternatives the customer even considers, the greater your pricing premium.

Principle 3: *The producer with the lowest-cost structure wins in a commodity market.* To avoid losing to such a producer you can become the only supplier of desired benefits in an existing or new-to-market category and then, by definition, you are no longer in a commodity market. As the sole supplier, your profits will grow as customers gain more value for themselves. To achieve this status, however, the customers' price premium for the unique benefits must be less than their value to your customer. Otherwise, you have not increased value to your customer.

Sports teams that win year after year rarely focus solely on individual talents. Rather, their consistent victories reflect a great *system* that works at every facet of the game. They know the importance of picking the right talent, developing it, training it, creating a powerful bond of teamwork, making strategic trades, designing great offensive strategies, and building a defense that can stop any other team's offense. Add in creative marketing and development, and you have a great franchise. It's great, that is, until another team finds the weak-

EXPLOITING STRATEGIC DIFFERENTIATION

The three economic principles for a strategically differentiated business discussed earlier can also help you understand the conditions that have to exist to generate higher sustained profits and increased demand. These conditions underscore the fact that building a strategically differentiated business is not easy, nor is it something you can decide on once and then forget.

A strategically differentiated business earns higher returns when the following conditions hold:

1. The customer genuinely gains additional value from how you are different.
2. The incremental value the customer derives from you exceeds your cost to create the differentiated position.
3. Competitors cannot copy you without significant ongoing financial consequences.
4. You continue to make changes that further increase customer value.

nesses in the team's strategy and exploits them by hiring away talent, creating a stronger defense, and building offensive strength. That is why any organization needs to renew itself regularly as external conditions change.

The same is true for differentiation in business. If your focus is only on an individual product or service offering, you are not developing a system that wins year after year. In fact, great products or services can even die if the overall system they are part of does not support differentiation and innovation. A strategically differentiated business is like a great sports team—it goes far beyond the functional attributes of an offering or a player.

A business is strategically differentiated when it—not an individual product or service—is designed, constructed, and managed to provide target customers with higher value offerings (tangible and intangible benefits less direct and indirect costs) that competitors cannot profitably match. A strategically differentiated business will not only offer new-to-market categories, it will also bring higher value to its most mature categories. If it cannot accomplish the latter, it will dramatically divert resources from these mature categories and likely exit the market.

ELIMINATE OPERATIONAL INEFFICIENCIES

There is a limit to how much you can get in terms of extra price from strategic differentiation. If you get to the point where your price premium over the competition offsets the value of your higher benefits, you've gone too far, and customers become indifferent regarding you and the lower-priced competitor. This reasoning is why you must always keep your eye on being operationally efficient. No customer will pay you for inefficiencies. Inefficiencies lower customer value if passed through in price or lower your profits if not passed through. Highly successful companies are therefore both strategically differentiated and operationally efficient. But their cost containment efforts must increase or not reduce customers' perceived value of their offerings.

ADVERTISING IS NOT STRATEGIC DIFFERENTIATION

Be wary of marketing service organizations that offer to do something for their customers they cannot really do. Examples include advertising agencies and marketing and branding gurus who claim to differentiate their clients' businesses through unique positioning. Positioning is not strategic differentiation. However, positioning can be an essential tool for the company that is already strategically differentiated.

Positioning is finding the place in the customer's mind where he or she houses your company or its offering. The goal is to be top-of-mind—get considered and establish a strong image that will lead customers to buy from you and remain loyal to you.

This communications role is where positioning serves a strategically differentiated business. You must communicate your unique value proposition to your target market and why that value proposition is better. And since customers are bombarded by messages 24/7, you must find the right message with an effective hook that leads them to want to learn more.

Advertising and other communication positioning, however, is not strategic differentiation. Ad agencies (a.k.a. branding consulting professionals and communications firms) will help you tell your story well, but they are unlikely to teach you what you have to do to create that story in the first place. Communication positioning is to strategic differentiation what painting a house is to its design and construction. No matter how great the paint job, it cannot hide the flaws of a home that is poorly designed and constructed or faces a crumbling foundation because the earth changed under it.

Worse, the ad agency working with your marketing department may identify differentiated features and associated benefits and lead you to think you have escaped the quicksand of commodity competition. If the differentiated features are not backed by a strategically differentiated business model, the law of nemesis (everyone will follow a good thing) will set you on the slippery slope and head you toward, then off, the survival mode cliff.

Use strategic differentiation to escape survival mode and earn higher profits.

Too many businesspeople feel they cannot affect their market. They assume that specific supply and demand curves exist for their company and industry that are beyond their influence other than by cutting costs so as to compete on price. Nevertheless, creating a unique offering by strategically differentiating your business can actually shift supply and demand curves favorably, enabling you to sell more at the same or higher prices. Strategic differentiation increases demand at every price, as more customers are attracted to your higher perceived value and it constricts supply. Offering a truly unique set of benefits increases your value relative to the competition, and customers will pay more for your offering.

If you remember only one thing from this book, please remember this: *Strategic differentiation of your business brings consistently higher returns than making cost-cutting process improvements or adding product features that competitors can readily match.*

One of the best examples of business model innovation is Apple Computer. Rather than putting all its resources into price battles with Dell in the personal computer (PC) market through cost cutting, Apple created a PC that looked like a piece of art and worked as easily as a familiar product, and then leveraged its skills at elegant and ergonomic design of electronic technology products by moving into the MP3 and cell phone business. All of its products are superior because of its underlying business model and its focus on offering the easiest to use, design-driven products.

Beginning the Journey: Taking the First Steps in Developing a Strategically Differentiated Business Model

Developing a new business model that is strategically differentiated doesn't happen overnight. The remaining steps of the *Beyond Price* process will help you flush out the necessary details. To get started on the journey, however, you have to change the mind-set of your business's leaders. We recommend that you address six issues with your leadership team:

1. Review each of the Economics 101 principles for commodity markets, and discuss how they apply to specific offerings of your company and your industry and how they are currently trapping you in highly price-competitive markets.

2. Use your financial reports to estimate how much of your revenue is from products or service categories that are already commodities or are quickly becoming commodities.

3. Discuss which customer groups, categories, or products or services are most commodity-like—that is, where purchasing decisions are made solely or almost solely on price. How did these market conditions arise for your company? (Consider customer, competitor, and company actions as well as technology, economic, and social changes.)

4. Discuss where, if at all, your products or services are free from commodity competition. Where have you broken out of or avoided commodity competition? What is different about those customer groups, categories, or individual offerings?

5. Ask if anyone on the team has examples of companies that have broken out of a commodity market or rarely compete on price. Do not restrict yourself to businesses in your market or even similar markets. Look for examples from any industry that can serve as role models.

6. Discuss what forces in your markets will create more commodity pressures going forward.

Deal with change.

Although your company's leaders may be concerned about its future, that doesn't necessarily mean that they are open to change—especially the magnitude of change required to break out of commodity markets or to steer in the opposite direction if you are headed toward commodity status.

There is usually tremendous doubt and resistance at the start of a transformation process. Although leaders are not blind, they may be unwilling to see. Although they are not ignorant, they may be unwilling to learn.

Leaders of established companies are likely to want to wait out the economy, hoping for an upturn that will create excess demand and acceptable profits, even in commodity markets. Fear of change may have turned into a strong belief that you cannot change conditions that create hardships for your company. The core belief is, "We can outlast this through our steady and heroic efforts to cut costs, make line extensions, improve packaging, or enhance service levels."

Furthermore, in many cases, business leaders have been measuring themselves against other companies in their industry—not against what is truly possible in their industry. And, if no one in the industry is strategically clever, the deep-seated belief that nothing can change is even stronger. Leaders whose companies are doing better than others in their industry may become smug, even though the organization is stuck in survival mode.

In a start-up company, leaders often believe they will be first to the market with their idea, and therefore need not worry about price-driven competition. They think the game is all about proving the technology or product concept, and not about establishing a unique business model with a differentiated market position. The high level of risk they are taking leads them to not recognize that their technology may become a commodity in less time than it takes to achieve their personal and business desires. Or, they forget that a company with only one product may never achieve the scale required for an IPO.

Some leaders will, unlike their peers, be full of hope for a better day. This is not grounded in a realistic plan to create better outcomes. Rather, it is a hope that they can use the power of their position or personality to create change in the company. Often, the change that is envisioned is more one of improving the effectiveness of the current business model rather than designing a brand-new one.

You may also run into resistance that sounds something like this: "Well, what this book says is fine in theory, but the authors have no idea of what is happening in our industry (or area of the country or type of ownership). It's not like anything they have seen. They're talking about an economy that no longer exists." It's true that we can't as authors address every situation in every industry, but remember that commoditization is like gravity: The economic principles affect everyone in exactly the same way. You will need to remind peers that economic principles are just that—truths that shape all markets. And you will need to draw some parallels between transformation stories in *Beyond Price* or other business literature and your business.

Finally, some colleagues will push back because their fear of failure in trying to change closes their minds to the possibility of change. Be patient. The eight steps in this book will slowly chip away at ingrained beliefs and fears. Eventually, you and other leaders will recall the lessons of this chapter and use it as proof that new strategies could, in fact, succeed in getting your business out of the quicksand of commodity markets.

That said, remember the Finfrock story from the introduction. Eventually, it became clear to Robert that some current leaders were simply not willing to change how they did their work in order to support the company's new direction. Because the stakes were so high, he eventually had to make the tough call to replace two managers. Obviously, it's not a step to be undertaken lightly, but you need to know it's a possibility if you are serious about accomplishing transformational change. Give leaders every opportunity to change, but in the end, do what is right for the company as a whole.

Conclusion

Creating the conditions in your organization that can switch your thinking from a commodity mentality to competing as a strategically differentiated *company* is no easy feat. And you can be sure that coworkers will not change if they see no need or opportunity to do so. The answer rests in unearthing new, attractive, and actionable insights about customers, markets, competitors, and your company's performance in its markets. Creating those insights is the subject of the next two steps. Step 2 discusses the need to adopt a new lens for your external assessment. We call this moving from being customer driven to being market driven. Step 3 provides a framework for using this new lens to surface previously invisible or discounted risks and exciting new growth and differentiation opportunities.

STEP 1 KEY POINTS

Understand the root cause of your problem; start working to develop a *Beyond Price* mentality.

Desired goal: Your team understands that commodity markets are the result of economic forces that can be reversed if you change how you do business.

Keys to success:

✓ Assume markets are changeable.

✓ Learn from other companies how to break out of commodity competition even if they are not in your industry. The economic principles remain the same.

✓ Strategic differentiation of your company comes before
  ▪ *Branding of your offering(s)*
  ▪ *Communication of benefits your customers receive*
  ▪ *Communication of your advantages that ensure that you can deliver on the promised benefits*

✓ Be open to the possibility that there is a better way to do business in your industry.

Doing everything right is not always the right thing to do.

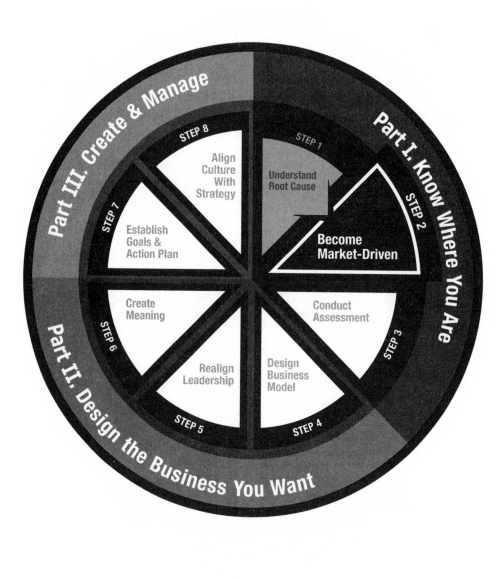

Step 2

Forget Customer Driven; Become Market Driven

Customer satisfaction is vital. But satisfied customers do not ensure your future success.

Ray and his team were perplexed. Despite significant growth in the number of in-office medical procedures performed in the United States, sales of their disposable medical products (used in physician offices) were flat. Why weren't sales growing? Interviews with the company's dealers provided no insights: The dealers reported that the company's products were holding onto their market share.

The only explanation that Ray's team could come up with for the disparity between their flat sales and the market growth was that there had been a change in product usage. Ray and his managers assumed that although their products were designed to be used once and then thrown out, some reuse must be going on. So they decided they should begin to explore development of semi-reusable offerings.

In fact, a far different trend explained the disparity between lack of growth in company sales and an increase in physician office procedures. But Ray's company missed seeing this trend because it was focused narrowly on its current products and existing distribution channel. Physician offices were consolidating and forming much closer affiliations with hospitals. Distributors that traditionally served hospitals were now targeting the large physician clinics as customers. Hospital buying groups were also targeting large clinics as customers.

In short, the disparity Ray's team had observed came because the market growth had occurred through a sales channel of which they weren't aware. A growing physician segment was no longer buying products from traditional distribution channels—the ones Ray's company served.

By the time Ray and his team identified what had happened, an upstart competitor had secured exclusive contracts with the hospital buying groups for the disposable products Ray's company manufactured. Ray's company had unknowingly lost considerable market share. Worse, the competitor was now positioned with the fastest-growing part of the market. Getting lost share back would be a very expensive proposition.

Although Ray and his management team thought they were doing all the right things, and took positive action to determine why product sales were flat, they realized that not only were they still trapped in a commodity market but also that their served market was shrinking every day. The hard lesson they learned is that customer satisfaction is vital, but satisfied customers do not ensure your future success.

Some readers may judge Ray and his team as poor leaders. Had they talked with the end-user physicians, the team would have been more likely to spot the new distribution channel. True, but at the time, many physicians had their head in the sands about changes in the physician market. Although the distribution channel change is not hard to spot for some companies, there are other changes outside the scope of a core market that leaders fail to see such as a noncompetitor suddenly entering your market, leveraging skills and assets you wish your company had.

In other words, Ray's company isn't alone. It wasn't that long ago that customer satisfaction was the mantra of ultimate success. Look how times have changed! In most markets today, providing high customer satisfaction may get you considered but doesn't guarantee that you'll be selected. And it certainly doesn't guarantee customer loyalty.

In this chapter, we'll briefly review why being customer driven won't get you out of a commodity market, and also set the groundwork for developing a *market focus* that will. Market-driven companies will, as you'll see in Step 4, succeed by driving the market, as they will be creating new-to-market categories. Strategically differentiated companies are both market driven and market driving.

YOU ARE HERE

Link to previous step: However willing the leadership team is to define new strategies to break out of commodity competition, some shift must occur in leaders' thinking. The shift from customer driven to market driven accomplishes just that.

Expected outcome: The leadership team will change its focus from customer driven to market driven. The former places the customer at the center of the organization. The latter recognizes that while the customer satisfaction must remain vitally important, not all customers are strategic, and the task of leadership is to be market driven by staying abreast of market changes. This shift in focus will enable leaders to decide in later steps which customer groups are strategic and what offerings will win their loyalty. The leadership team also commits in this step to building a strong market-understanding process that parallels its financial-understanding process. The presence of strong market understanding is what keeps the company out of commodity market quicksand in years ahead.

Who is involved: The leadership team makes a commitment to build a strong market-understanding process. Others in the company will be involved in its design and still more will interface with the process.

Why this step is important: Leaders will never see the opportunities to make their companies truly differentiated if they focus on and listen only to their current customers. All employees should have a focus on current customers because that's how you stay in business today. But the company's leaders must be more broadly focused to ensure future success. Opportunities to meet the needs of new customer segments are only seen if the leadership team is focused on a much broader marketplace. *Indeed, the broader one's view, the more strategic insights and options there are.*

Why Customer Satisfaction Became a Commodity

The problem with focusing on customer satisfaction is found in the law of nemesis: "Everybody follows a good thing." Creating an advantage invites others to copy your business and therefore negates your advantage.

The past few decades have given us example after example of how becoming customer driven has helped businesses lower costs, win price premiums, and gain greater market share. The rest of us followed suit because we wanted the same results. As a consequence, doing this basic customer and quality work no longer offers a competitive advantage. And guess what? That means customers can purchase primarily on price, the very definition of a commodity market.

The bottom line is that even though we have dramatically increased customer value through our attention to quality and service, only the customer wins, because there is far less or no differentiation among acceptable suppliers. The dramatic changes in most markets, in response to information technology, industry and distribution channel consolidations, shareholder pressure, and global competition, is only making matters worse. Business's way of saying this is, "We seem to be providing more value and getting less and less for it." It is time to admit that the era of being customer driven is over. This does not mean to say that companies will not continue to focus on satisfying customers. Winning firms will do more than this, however.

BEING CUSTOMER FOCUSED INVOLVES THE FOLLOWING:

- Placing the customer at the center of the organization

- Improving and redesigning processes, products, and services to better service customers

- Responding to customers' demand for change (often initiated by seeing another supplier do something new) so as to retain satisfied customers

From Customer Driven to Market Driven: Listening to a Higher Voice

Companies that have successfully escaped a commodity market are those that have shifted from being customer driven first and foremost to being *market driven:* They have broadened their external focus so they can understand the forces at work in their market as a whole, and they make deliberate decisions about both *where* to compete and *how* they will stand out from the competition. They are still driving change to earn the delight and loyalty of their customers, but only in the context of strategically selected customer segments.

The key differences between market-driven and customer-driven companies are shown in Table 2.1. As a result of all this work, market-driven organizations delight strategic customers with what they need but could not articulate.

Understanding Why Being Market Driven Is Necessary for Escaping Commodity Competition

Developing a broader market awareness is a must if you want to get out of price-based commodity competition, for four primary reasons.

Customers don't always know what they really need.

If customers had the answer to what they really needed, that answer would become part of the criteria that must be met before they would even consider your offerings. Customers (and you'll hear their words repeated verbatim by your sales force) can articulate only what they want that they think is possible.

For example, FedEx defining overnight delivery was unexpected at the time. It brought benefits that redefined traditional delivery industry benefits as substandard, even though customers *appeared* to be satisfied *before* the new player entered the market.

Market-driven companies define their competition broadly through an expansive view of the market. They regularly ask, "How can we better serve the marketplace?"

TABLE 2.1 *Key differences between customer-driven and market-driven companies*

CHARACTERISTIC	CUSTOMER-DRIVEN ORGANIZATIONS	MARKET-DRIVEN ORGANIZATIONS
Customer research	■ Narrowly focused on current and lost customers and current competitors. ■ "Customer understanding" means asking customers what they want (and meeting those expressed needs).	■ Broadly focused on people and trends that create risks and opportunities. ■ "Customer understanding" means knowing what is needed but hasn't been asked for by current and potential customers, and investigating what is keeping customers from achieving their goals.
Market research process	■ Process is not well defined or managed. ■ Sales and marketing staff hold information rather than share it with the rest of the company. ■ Focus is on current customers in current markets unless there is a new product development effort targeted at a new customer group.	■ Well-defined and well-managed process for acquiring, interpreting, and using marketplace information in decisions. ■ Individuals throughout the company are involved in market understanding; all opinions balanced with marketing acting as interpreter. ■ Also seeks information about its 　□ Indirect competitors 　□ Suppliers 　□ Companies offering complementary products or services 　□ Customer's customer who may be a business or a consumer
Business scope	■ Narrow view of business scope (want to retain and build current customer base keeping current offerings). ■ Historical business scope is taken as a given, not a decision to be regularly examined. ■ Only move into new categories when business would be lost otherwise. ■ Business is defined by current customers.	■ Broad view of potential business scope (expand beyond current customer base and offering). ■ Approach "What business are we in?" as a strategic question. ■ Regularly evaluates the scope of offerings in terms of maximizing customer value. ■ Boundaries of business scope are defined by what the leadership team views as the best opportunities for building a differentiated business.

CHARACTERISTIC	CUSTOMER-DRIVEN ORGANIZATIONS	MARKET-DRIVEN ORGANIZATIONS
Product / service sphere	▪ Solution set is restricted to current products or services niches.	▪ Open to solutions that solve customer problems yet aren't current part of what the company does. ▪ Seeks new-to-market categories where there is no competition.
Culture	▪ Only listen to customers.	▪ Open to new ideas from multiple sources.
Basis of decision making	▪ Short-term perspective. ▪ Rarely gives up business to get business.	▪ Long-term perspective. ▪ Willing to give up business to secure more attractive business.
Process improvement focus	▪ Focus is on cost reductions and traditional quality improvements.	▪ Focus is on wherever firm builds its advantage, not just cost reductions.
Outwardly focused skill sets emphasized	▪ Relationship selling is emphasized.	▪ Market understanding and economic literacy throughout the firm is emphasized. ▪ Relationship selling is emphasized, with a goal of determining how to maximize value that customers receive.

Not all customers are equal.

Have you ever analyzed what percentage of revenues come from individual customers or market segments and compared this with how much it costs you to do business with them? When businesses perform this exercise, they learn that not all customers or segments are equally profitable. Most likely, there are some that represent the majority of your profits. Further, doing business with some of the other segments will *never* result in a profit. Now imagine segmenting your potential customer base on other criteria that differentiate one group from another.

Being market focused means you are making deliberate decisions about where you compete. This includes the market segments you serve, as well as the products and services you offer. It makes some customers, market segments, and offerings more strategic than others because you can better meet their needs and compete as one in a category of one rather than one of many.

AN EXAMPLE OF THE SHIFT TO MARKET DRIVEN

A plastic thermoform company served multiple markets with its own proprietary products and as a supplier to consumer goods product manufacturers. Although the company served many packaging markets, it held no leadership position in any one. It chose a new business model to focus on a few markets in which packaging could play a key role in demonstrating product features (e.g., a scissors package that lets a potential buyer feel the product's hand movement). At that time, a packaged-food company approached the thermoform company to invest in microwave packaging technology in return for the food company's business. In the past, the leadership team would make the investments the customer asked for, as the packaging company was customer driven; but this behavior created diffused investments and skill development. By turning down the food company (a nonstrategic customer) to invest more in strategic markets, the packaging company built a strong position in a narrower set of markets, a formula for more profitable growth.

All too often, companies think that casting a broad net will lead to more revenue growth because it will increase their potential market. This strategy is especially risky in consumer goods companies and B2B companies, like packaging, where there is no end of potential market segments for the industry's offering. In many industries, especially mature ones, a broad focus on *all* possible markets severely restricts your potential profitability, as you end up trying to be all things to all groups, a surefire recipe for never being truly the best for a narrower set of targets.

A broad focus undermines the organization's success, because each distinct marketplace has very different demands from companies that serve it. For example, large institutional food-service companies serving a national market have different needs from kitchen and dining product manufacturers than do small gourmet restaurants. Grade school students have different needs from textbook publishers than do graduate students. A company trying to serve too many divergent markets will dilute investments and focus, unless economies-of-scale advantages offset the advantages of focus.

A focus only on the battle for today's customers obscures risks and opportunities emerging in the broader market.

A customer-driven firm will not be prepared for the entry of a new competitor or an unexpected move from an existing one. In contrast, a market-driven firm has a broader perspective to analyze the risks and opportunities presented in an evolving marketplace.

As an example, consider how computer software and the Internet are transforming legal services. A group of lawyers, realizing that many law firms often do not understand how technology could revolutionize their industry, started an Internet law practice. They developed standardized formats and solutions to deliver a lower-cost and therefore higher-value alternative for routine corporate legal questions. They captured market share from larger traditional law firms.

Market-driven companies can enjoy the success inherent in being proactive rather than reactive in a changing market.

By the time your customers articulate new needs, there are already suppliers serving the market, ensuring commodity competition.

Even if you are regularly asking your customers what they want, so are your competitors. If your development agenda is focused solely on product enhancements or service changes requested by your customers, customer-driven competitors will meet this need sooner than or shortly after you.

For example, the movement of advanced composite technology, from defense to commercial manufacturing industries, will significantly affect many industries such as construction and packaging. It will be years before these new materials become standard. Nevertheless, the market-driven companies that are investing today to understand the production, design, and performance implications of the new technology will secure long-term success. Customer-driven companies that fail to assume this leadership role may become obsolete. Leaders who understand that the new composites benefit customers, even if those same customers do not yet understand this, will become more successful and will earn considerable market share from firms focused only on customers' current satisfaction.

Market-driven companies look at the larger context around their customers or engage in activities that allow them to observe rather than solely listen to customers. As a result, they gain ideas that lead to truly proprietary offerings.

Recognizing Indicators That You Should Become Market Driven

The need to replace being customer driven with being market driven occurs at different times in different industries. You should become market driven when

- Competition is increasingly based on price.
- The technology underlying your offering is maturing.
- There are growing risks of companies from outside your industry biting off an attractive niche.
- A new technology must change significantly to attract a broader acceptance.
- Technology changes could fundamentally alter your industry.
- Other companies can vertically integrate into your industry to improve their growth prospects or better meet their customers' needs.

From a company's perspective, the need to shift from customer driven to market driven generally comes at a defined stage in its evolution. In the early stage, the need to survive drives the company's actions. Proving its products or services concept, its technology, or its operating approach is at the heart of management's interests. From there, the company becomes sales driven. Later, when sales growth begins to taper off, it becomes increasingly profit driven.

A customer-driven culture may have been part of the company's culture from the start or it may evolve during the sales- and profit-driven stages as leadership realizes the link between satisfied customers and ongoing, profitable business. But at some point, the company's growth in both sales and profits comes to a halt. In some industries, sales may actually start to decline, at which point, in order to be successful, the company *must* become market driven. It must redefine where and how it will compete and, internally, what it must excel at to secure leadership positions in targeted markets.

High-technology start-ups are realizing the critical value of being market driven. They increasingly realize that a new technology can serve multiple markets. Understanding the breadth of markets and picking the one that is the best fit helps to create victories before investment dollars disappear. The broad market knowledge also helps them identify future products and market applications once they have proven their technology's first application.

The Importance of a Market-Understanding Process

You become market driven by building a strong *market-understanding process* that enables you to acquire, interpret, and use market information in any decisions that have market or customer implications. A market-understanding process should operate like the financial-understanding process all companies have. The acquisition, interpretation, and use of financial information in company decisions is treated as a core process. The "deliverable" of the financial-understanding process is *not* the internal financial information per se, but rather, better decisions that affect the organization's ability to meet its financial goals. Thus, training the management team to interpret and use internal information effectively is a key part of this financial-understanding process.

Few of the conditions for financial information exist with regard to market information. In most companies, the market-understanding process is left to the serendipity of individuals. The process changes as the members of the marketing and sales departments change. The implicit process will be as good or as bad as individual sales and marketing managers and their commitment to market understanding.

Imagine your company without a *strong* financial-understanding process. Now begin to think about the effect of a *weak* market-understanding process, one characterized by the following:

- When marketing and salespeople quit or retire, their knowledge of the market leaves with them; it is no longer "housed" in the company.

- Marketing or sales departments do not necessarily receive information that comes into the company from other sources.

- No one formally oversees the process of interpreting and using market information effectively.

- The organization limits management effort and investment in acquiring market information.

- There is no process to improve the use of market information in decision making.

Paralleling the financial-understanding process, the market-understanding process embraces acquisition, interpretation, and use of information in decision making. Market information is much broader than just the measure of customer satisfaction. The focus is not only on customers and offerings but also on the market, competitors, and external trends (economic, demographic, societal, technological, and institutional, for example). It includes an understanding of how things may change in the future, not just snapshots of today. Finally, it takes a very broad view of potential market space for your company. In other words, you look far past the market space defined by current customers and current offerings.

Absent a well-defined market-understanding process, the *urgent* will drive out the *important* in day-to-day activities, and the company will move back to being internally focused. Also, without a desire to become more market driven, it will be very difficult for your leadership to engage in a strategic assessment (Step 3) in a way that generates fresh strategic insights and promising new opportunities.

Beginning the Market-Understanding Process

Becoming a market-driven firm is not an overnight event. Odds are your company currently lacks many of the elements of a market-understanding process as already described.

The first step is *making the commitment to become market driven* by building a market-understanding process. As you go through the remaining steps, you will be able to identify information you need about the market you are in and potential markets into which you could move. You can use those insights to help you start defining objectives for improving your market understanding.

KEY ELEMENTS OF A FINANCIAL-UNDERSTANDING AND MARKET-UNDERSTANDING PROCESS

- The financial-understanding process belongs to the company, not to individuals in the company. That means it is built into the way the company does business and can survive, even if some individuals are gone. The same is true for the market-understanding process.

- Financial management develops policies and procedures and ensures that they are followed consistently month to month, and staff person to staff person. The chief marketing officer does the same.

- The financial staff do a lot more than acquire and report financial information. They design and manage an internal information process that encompasses the acquisition, interpretation, and use of financial information concerning the sales, costs, assets, liabilities, variances, and profits of the company. The marketing staff addresses market information concerning competitors, external changes impacting markets, customer segments, etc.

- Employees in other departments both participate in the process (i.e., generate information fed into financial or marketing databanks) and/or are beneficiaries of the process (such as getting budget limits from the financial-understanding process or competitor profiles from the market-under- standing process).

- The job of the CFO is to ensure that the process goals are aligned with, and contribute to, overall organizational goals, and that the financial-understanding process is efficient and effective. He or she oversees improvements in the process that result in better-quality information, gained faster or at lower cost and used more effectively in decision making. To accomplish this, the CFO establishes process goals, measures performance, and invests in process improvements (e.g., new systems, consultants, training, etc.). The chief marketing officer adopts a similar role regarding the market-understanding process.

THE LEADERSHIP TEAM NEEDS AN EXPANSIVE VIEW OF WHERE TO COMPETE

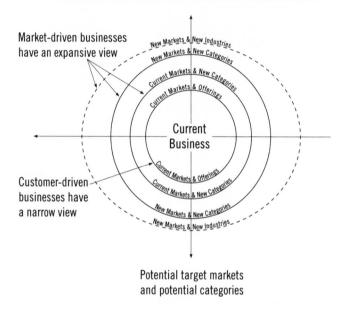

Market-driven businesses have an expansive view

New Markets & New Industries
New Markets & New Categories
Current Markets & New Categories
Current Markets & Offerings

Current Business

Current Markets & Offerings
Current Markets & New Categories
New Markets & New Categories
New Markets & New Industries

Customer-driven businesses have a narrow view

Potential target markets and potential categories

FIGURE 2.1 *Comparison of customer-driven and market-driven companies*

THE IMPORTANCE OF LEADERSHIP

Managers who foster change and renewal on a daily basis lead market-driven firms. They lead by developing a keen understanding of the status quo and challenging it regularly. They demonstrate a passion for innovative people, ideas, and environments. They are the managers who hire people who are not cast in a single mold; rather, these new hires bring a new and different set of gifts to the team.

Leaders at market-driven firms know that marketing is too important to leave (only) to the marketing department. Market-driven organizations involve all departments in making market-related strategic decisions, enabling the entire organization to move efficiently, effectively, and speedily in chosen directions, thereby advancing enduring success.

Leaders at market-driven firms understand the importance of making strategic assessments. In fact, strategic assessments are among the most important tools that market-driven firms employ to obtain a realistic, honest understanding of their business and its position in its markets. We will discuss strategic assessments in detail in the next chapter.

Get started.

To begin the transformation, discuss the following questions with your leadership team:

- Is becoming a differentiated company (versus remaining a commodity supplier) critical to our long-term success? (See Step 1 for a discussion of differentiated versus commodity supplier.) Why or why not?
- Do we have the market understanding we need to accomplish that transition? (Tip: Review the description of a market-driven company in Table 2.1 and rate yourself against each item.)
- What do we need to change to make the market-understanding process a strategic process for our company?
- Who should be the owner of this process? Who else should be involved? Do we have a talented chief marketing officer? If not, do we need one?
- How should we measure the effectiveness of our market-understanding process?
- What improvement goals make sense for our company's market-understanding process?

After this discussion, develop a plan for moving forward. Which elements of the market-understanding process can you put in place immediately? Which will take longer to plan and implement?

Handle the change from customer driven to market driven.

It's one thing to accept the concept of market driven. It's quite another to make the change. Following is advice on how to proceed:

1. *Understand the magnitude of what you're asking people to do—and the enormous threat it poses.* The move from customer driven to market driven can be very threatening to leaders, not unlike switching from one trapeze to another. Letting go is scary. Remaining customer driven is rather easy—leaders feel they know the name of the game and how to play it. Achieving success becomes only an issue of execution. Asking leaders to move to market driven, where the leadership team redefines what is required for success, raises fear of failure.

2. *Acknowledge that a customer focus worked well in the past.* Many of your leaders will be focused on understanding and satisfying current customer needs, and they will have stopped looking more broadly at the market. These leaders focus only on those needs that customers can articulate, rather than on undeclared needs. You won't get these leaders to change by criticizing what they have done in the past. Rather, acknowledge that their approach has served the company but that it is no longer sufficient in today's marketplace. Involve them in identifying what other areas need to be explored (lost and potential customers, current and potential competitors, new technologies). Challenge them to think about how they would go about identifying needs that current customers cannot articulate.

3. *Resist attempts to pigeonhole "market understanding" in the sales department.* Leaders, especially in B2B markets, sometimes charge their sales departments with the responsibility of market understanding. They may not see that sales representatives are just one part of a well-designed market-understanding process. Relying exclusively on the sales force to understand the market will give you a biased and extremely short-term view of opportunities and risks. The sales force, rightfully so, spends all its time with organizations that will buy more product today. They do not see the larger market. Companies with marketing departments and even market research staff must remember the inherent limitations of information and suggestions from the sales force.

4. *Constantly reinforce the message that a business rooted in current customers cannot thrive.* There are a number of ways to move past this resistance.

First, remind associates that satisfied customers will switch suppliers and brands as soon as someone offers a better deal. Second, customers do not know everything, only what they would buy today if available. And they have likely shared even this limited information with your competition. Keeping leaders' eyes on the market will ensure that your company is the one that comes up with the truly better offerings, not just a lower price. Third, help leaders accept that a market-understanding process is as vital as the company's financial-understanding processes. The latter keeps score. The former creates the insights that help you win the game of business.

Conclusion

Being customer driven is Management 101. Breaking out of and staying out of commodity competition requires going beyond Management 101. Becoming market driven does not replace a customer orientation. Rather, it broadens the lens with which you explore the multiple forces that can shape your business positively or negatively, depending on your willingness to observe and change. With this broader focus you'll anticipate and capitalize on changes happening in your customers' environments that will move you out of commodity competition.

STEP 2 KEY POINTS

Forget customer driven; become market driven.

Desired goals:

- ✓ Understand the limitations of customer-driven strategies.
- ✓ Commit your leadership and company to becoming more market driven.
- ✓ Make a commitment to build a stronger market-understanding process.

Keys to success:

- ✓ Suspend your belief that customers have all the answers.
- ✓ Recognize that external information is like oxygen—too little can have a very adverse effect.
- ✓ Foster diversity in people and ideas. Recognize that everyone in the company has a role in understanding the market and unearthing breakthrough ideas to break out of commodity competition.

Customer satisfaction is vital. But satisfied customers do not ensure your future success.

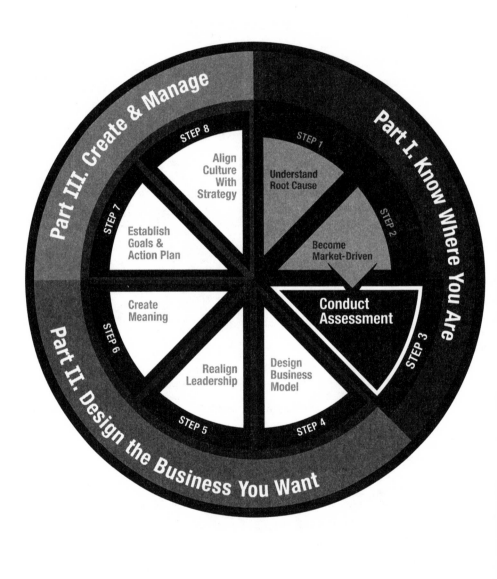

Step 3

Conduct a Strategic Assessment

Become a consultant to your own business to capture fresh market insights into new risks and opportunities.

Jeff was an outstanding manager, hired as CEO of a small, privately held company with a strong niche position in the R&D laboratory market. Improvements in manufacturing, sales, and marketing had not returned expected improvements in the bottom line. An investigation helped Jeff's team understand why.

The company had started out being a supplier of upholstery services to manufacturers of equipment and furniture used in business settings. It had then begun making an R&D laboratory stool, which the company decided to sell under its own brand name. The company had earned a name for itself for this ergonomically designed niche product. Margins were much higher on this product than its other offerings, leading the company to begin manufacturing more major pieces of R&D laboratory furniture.

By the time Jeff was brought on board, the company had not only developed its own higher-end laboratory furniture products but also acquired a company producing a high-end niche electronic test instrument used in selected R&D laboratory settings and a company selling simple and basic supplies used in R&D labs.

An evaluation of all the risks and opportunities facing the business disputed the company's belief that it had a viable business model built around serving R&D labs. In fact, the company was in three entirely separate businesses: (1) the original branded product and other laboratory furnishings business, (2) the R&D lab supplies business, and (3) a niche electronic test instrument business. All of these could loosely be described as laboratory products, but their key decision makers, skill requirements, and the appropriate distribution channels differed greatly across all three businesses. With limited resources, the company could not grow all three businesses into sustainable market-leading businesses. This assessment helped Jeff's leadership team identify the business within which it could best grow and earn a leadership position. Through divestiture of the other businesses, Jeff built a thriving business.

This broad investigation of all the factors affecting a business is called a *strategic assessment.* Performing this kind of assessment is critical to escaping commodity markets as it allows you to develop new insights into the risks and opportunities facing your organization.

It is impossible to create a differentiated business model when your leadership team is so focused on operational and financial performance that it has no idea where the road leads. Like Dorothy's yellow-brick road, leaders assume their road will end in the right place. Unfortunately, often such assumptions lead to survival mode. And as the old saying goes: *If we do not turn around, we just might end up where we are headed.*

To create a road map that identifies routes out of and away from commodity markets, you need to begin with a realistic assessment of where you are and the direction in which you are headed. This will help you identify alternative options that will lead to a better future than the status quo offers.

The strategic assessment is a process for creating new and actionable insights in your business regarding its risks and opportunities. It answers a series of questions about the business, causing your management to look at the business from a less-biased, more-external, and longer-term perspective. Done effectively, a strategic assessment focuses management on the sustainability of the business over four to six *years* or more, not just the next four *quarters*.

In this step, we'll walk you through four secrets to conducting a good strategic assessment. We'll then share ten questions that are written to force you to think *strategically* about the risks and opportunities your business is facing, about where your business is, and about where it could be. These questions will push you beyond the same old answers you may have gotten in the past.

Since every company is unique in its origins, history, operations, and marketplace, there is no universal pathway for getting the answers to these ten questions. Rather, we'll present guidelines to help you develop your own plan, including a discussion of internal and external information you may already have on hand, what new information you may need, and what sources you may want to seek out. We will also give you a tool for recording risks and opportunities.

The step closes with some reminders about resistance you may encounter, as you do this work, and tips for working through that resistance. Note that you

---

YOU ARE HERE

Link to previous steps: Your leadership team should now understand the market forces that cause commodity competition (Step 1). It should also be more attuned to the external marketplace with its new market-driven lens (Step 2). Now it's time to gather fresh insights about your organization's risks and opportunities. The strategic assessment provides the leadership team with an organizing framework for reexamining the marketplace.

Expected outcome: You will gain deeper and more realistic insights into your organization's risks and the implications of the status quo. The new insights will also create new, actionable opportunities.

Who is involved: The management team takes the lead, supplemented with creative and insightful associates who can offer unique views of the organization and its markets. In addition, it's helpful to include representatives from noncompetitor partner organizations that serve a key role in making or distributing your offering. A nonemployee board member can also be very helpful.

Why this step is important: The same old ideas will lead to the same old results. The questions in this chapter will help you take a fresh look at your business.

WHY NOT DEFINE A VISION FIRST?

Many business advisers will tell you to first define your desired destination, also known as your vision, and then develop strategies to reach that destination. We believe that conducting a strategic assessment, and using the market insights you gain to set a new direction through business model innovation, is the essential first step. An honest, thorough assessment can reveal destinations you may not have thought possible or even thought of at all! Also, if the leadership team is brutally honest, the process of creating a strategic assessment will accurately identify the risks and opportunities most crucial for future action. These insights will lead the leadership team to be more open and far-reaching when they talk about a desired vision. And your coworkers, in seeing a bridge to a better future, will be more willing to craft an inspiring vision. Their enthusiasm for the vision will determine the speed with which you reach it; wait to discuss vision until there is cause for newfound enthusiasm due to a new business model.

---

may want to skip the detailed descriptions of how you answer the ten questions until you've finished reading *Beyond Price* and are ready to start Step 3.

Above all, Step 3 is an exploratory, information-gathering step. Instructions for synthesizing and integrating what you've learned, and for using those insights to develop a new business model, come in Step 4. In the meantime, be broad in your thinking and your approach. Expand the horizons of what you think is possible. And trust that collectively your organization knows a lot more about your business and its markets than you may have observed in past strategy meetings. "One plus one equals three" when coworkers face new questions about their business and there is a process to answer these questions as a team.

Learning the Four Secrets to a Breakthrough Strategic Assessment

If you approach developing a new competitive strategy for your organization with the same people, at the same time of the year (typically before budgets), and with the same information (the inside view of the marketplace) that you've always used, don't expect a new, winning competitive strategy to emerge. You will merely spend time confirming that you are already doing everything you possibly can for success in the market within which you are already competing. You'll still be trapped in your commodity markets or stuck on the slippery slopes toward them, which will breed cynicism and dampen motivation to change. How, therefore, should you approach the strategic assessment process?

There are four secrets to creating a successful strategic assessment.

1. *When* you conduct the strategic assessment

2. *How* you conduct the assessment

3. *Who* is involved in the assessment

4. *What* you learn from the assessment

SECRET 1: WHEN? *Start any time except during preparation of annual budgets.*

Too often, companies make strategic decisions while preparing the annual budget. This is exactly the *wrong* time to engage in this type of work! The budget process itself immediately focuses managers' attention on the rest of the current fiscal year and the next fiscal year. Therefore, managers' thinking is extremely tactical.

Creating a strategically differentiated business model requires more than a one-time course correction. You must make strategic assessment an ongoing process, because the market will be constantly changing. That is why it is best to engage in strategic assessment work at the very start of a fiscal year after budgets have been established.

Also, your ability to perform an effective assessment will improve with time. In the first year, for example, you may be working with limited information, using the assessment process to establish objectives. This will enable you to do more thorough assessments, and get better information, each following year. It is common for a solid strategically differentiated business model to begin to emerge after two years, with further advancements emerging in later years.

BE A CONSULTANT TO YOUR OWN BUSINESS

The mental image you want for this step is being a consultant to your own organization. Dismiss your ego and all its defensiveness and start assessing what is strong and what is weak about your company. Being open to alternative options is essential. Conclusions such as "We did that before and it did not work" should be avoided. To be truly effective, your strategic assessment must not begin with a specific destination in mind, or you will lose the opportunity to discover destinations that you might not have imagined or even thought possible.

SECRET 2: HOW? *Act like an outsider critically evaluating your own business.*

Insanity, Einstein noted, is doing the same thing over and over and expecting different results. If you do this strategic assessment the same way you've made all your previous strategic assessments, you'll likely end up stuck where you are now. This is where the mental image of being a consultant to your own business is critical.

The most difficult aspect will be looking *within* your business with new eyes. You probably think you already have a good idea of what's happening inside your company. And maybe you do. But you have to act as if you don't have a clue and challenge yourself to shed preconceived notions and assumptions masking as facts and listen to others who can offer different perspectives. The ten questions this step poses will help you see with new eyes. This step will preclude your team merely repeating the tried and true list of risks and opportunities.

Getting a new external view is critical as well. Without external market information, it is highly unlikely your strategic assessment will offer rich new insights. Good information from the outside will both shake confidence in the *status quo* and identify opportunities not previously seen or deemed achievable. Don't let the cost (in research expenditures or your people's time) keep you from getting this outside information. Undiscovered market insights or finding things out simply in due course will be more costly to your bottom line, since this makes you merely customer driven rather than market driven.

SECRET 3: WHO? *The leadership team should be complemented by new people who bring new ways of seeing.*

The same old people are likely to come up with the same old ideas. A leadership team entrenched in commodity markets is likely to be wearing rose-colored glasses that make everything about today look "not so bad." Other leaders may have become so pessimistic that the best strategy might be right in front of them and they refuse to see it. Or, if they do see it, they deem the strategy too hard to accomplish because it strips away their security blanket of comfortable, established practices and procedures.

So the first lesson about doing a strategic assessment is that you can't rely solely on your existing leadership team. The second is that you can't delegate it to someone else. All too often, CEOs delegate the strategic assessment work to the marketing and sales department without the rest of the senior team being involved. Although this may be efficient, it is not effective. "Marketing is too important to leave to the marketing department," as David Packard used to say about strategic marketing decisions.

For the strategic assessment to help your company break free from the quicksand of survival mode, you must rely on the entire senior team *and* make new people part of the process. Bringing together a well-rounded assessment team is critical.

Here are some new people you might want to include:

- Outsiders who have a strong stake in your future
- A consultant from outside your industry who can see things without the biases built into your industry's culture
- Marketing or CEO talents from companies you admire
- Individuals from various levels in the organization who see the organization from different vantage points

Remember that you want to get insights from outside your company. That means, in part, turning things around and conducting an assessment as if you are sitting in your competitor's chair. From that vantage point you can more realistically look at your company's true vulnerabilities and anticipate competitive moves that could put you at risk. At the same time, you will examine your competition's vulnerabilities to identify new opportunities. To get these outsider-like insights, it helps to have people in the group—such as new hires or outsiders who know you and your competitors—who will enlighten the conversation.

Finally, because an analysis of inside information will be important in the process, make sure your CFO is a key participant.

SECRET 4: WHAT? *Understand the longer-term risks and opportunities facing your business.*

In this step, you are committing time to doing a true strategic assessment: bringing together a diverse group to help gather information from a variety of sources and using that information to answer difficult questions about your company. All of that effort will be in vain unless you push for deeper market insights than you've relied on in the past. Remember, the goal is to unlock strategic insights, identify long-term risks, and unearth previously invisible opportunities.

As you conduct the strategic assessment, use a tracking form like that provided in Table 3.4 on page 96 to capture your insights.

Performing a Strategic Assessment

Doing a thorough strategic assessment takes time and dedication, but the payoff is well worth the effort. The goal here is to get information and insights that will help you identify and prioritize risks and opportunities associated with both your current business model and new business models that offer the chance to break out of competing primarily on price.

Getting those insights is a matter of answering ten strategic questions.

1. Why are our sales what they are?
2. Do we or could we have a unique competency that benefits a group of customers?
3. What factors drive our profitability?
4. Where do we compete, and what are the pros and cons of where we compete?
5. Are we currently strategically differentiated from our competition?

6. What sacrifices and compromises must customers make to use our industry's offerings that we might be able to help them avoid?

7. What are the strong and weak positions in our current portfolio of offerings and markets?

8. Is the whole of our business worth more than its individual parts?

9. What is the larger value chain of which we are a part, and is the overall value chain well designed to deliver maximum value to target groups of customers?

10. What is changing externally, and how will that affect our orthodoxies about our markets and our business?

The logic behind this sequence is that you want to ground yourself in a realistic understanding of where you are today (customer perceptions, capabilities, competitive position), and then expand to look at a broader concept of your market. This combination of views will help you reevaluate your target markets, the scope of your offerings, and what you offer, or could offer, better than the competition or without any competition.

The remainder of this section walks through the ten questions. Afterward, we'll give you directions on how to develop a plan for getting the answers and insights you need from these questions.

Readers of this book have vastly different businesses. Some create products and services purchased by other businesses, and others create consumer products and services. Some companies are a single business unit and other companies, likely larger in size, are composed of multiple business units. Some businesses offer a single category, and others offer multiple categories. Use the ten questions in ways that work best for your business. More complex companies may, for example, want to answer different questions at the category level, product level,

---

CEO INVOLVEMENT IN STRATEGIC ASSESSMENTS

One final point to remember: A strong leader is needed to push this process forward. The CEO or general manager must be the champion of producing a strong strategic assessment, but someone else can be charged with facilitating the process.

and business unit level. Consumer goods companies may want to answer each question from the perspective of sales to retailers and then sales to the end consumer. Business product companies may want to answer different questions from the perspective of their direct customer and then their customers' customers and distribution channel partners.

You may want to skip to page 88 (Getting Answers), returning to the following sections about how to answer each of the ten strategic questions *after* you've completed reading *Beyond Price*.

1. Why are our sales what they are?

This question is designed to help you document risks and opportunities related to revenue factors. Although most firms can explain an operating variance down to the dollar, very few can explain why their revenue is what it is. They do not understand when sales fall short of or exceed forecast, or even how this variance could emerge. Market-driven companies, however, understand exactly what is driving their sales and the best leverage points for improving them.

Measurement of what is driving revenue is essential to growing it. Why? Because the only thing a business can control is what it can accurately measure.

Sales can be broken down into a number of components using a simple equation, one that can be applied to each product or service offering.

> **REVENUE = Served market size × Awareness rate ×**
> **Consideration rate × Win rate × Relative purchases per customer**
> **× Relative selling price of your offering**

Now that we've drawn the equation on the blackboard, let's take a look at what each element of the equation means:

- *Served market size* is market size (in dollars) times the percentage of the market you can potentially serve with your current offering, channels, and geographic locations. Clearly, expanding the percentage of the market you serve is a key growth opportunity.

- *Awareness rate* is the percentage of the market you serve that is aware of your company. This is a vital measure of the effectiveness of your communications initiatives. Without awareness, there can be no sale.

Awareness is a fundamental driver of sales. Potential customers need to know *who you are* and *what you offer,* and *how to reach you.*

- *Consideration rate* is the percentage of those who are aware of you that are willing to consider your offering. This is a vital measure of whether you meet the basic requirements of customers and have satisfied past customers. Dissatisfied customers lower your consideration rate, as they will not consider you for future purchases. Differentiation will not increase revenue and gross margin percentages if you do not meet the basic requirements to be considered.

- *Win rate* is the percentage of those customers who consider your offering that actually buy it. The win rate measures your success against other qualified competitors. The win rate is a critical measure for understanding return on the total resources required to put together a proposal or bring a consumer product to the market. Low win rates reflect wasted resources. The win rate also sheds light on whether or not customers see your company as offering more value than other alternatives that meet minimum consideration requirements.

- *Relative purchase rate* is the average number of units that each of your customers purchases relative to the average units purchased by

---

THINK STRATEGICALLY

As you begin sifting through all the information you're about to gather, you want to be *thinking strategically,* adopting a broad perspective about your company and its markets. The broader the perspective you have, the broader the set of options you will be able to consider, and therefore the more room there is for good ideas to emerge. Coupling a broad and deep understanding of your customers (current, lost, and potential) with knowledge of what your company can or could do for them will allow you to find opportunities to address needs and solve problems the customers assumed could not be addressed. Solutions that eliminate the traditional compromises that customers experience in your industry, or that take on jobs your customer is delighted to be rid of, are at the heart of differentiation.

customers in your served market. This measure may be low if your offering does not meet many of the situational needs of your customer base.

- *Relative selling price of your offerings* is your average selling price per unit or contract value relative to the average in your served market.

Many companies lack data or have not tabulated it to analyze which factors are most important in driving their revenue changes. The payback to these data is insights into new opportunities to grow revenue and/or about additional risks you're facing. It is well worth the investment of financial or marketing staff resources to get the data. On the one hand, companies with high awareness and consideration rates but low win rates should dig deep into reasons why potential customers do not select them.

A food products manufacturer engaged in this exercise may realize it is trying to be all things to many different target markets, each with different taste, convenience, serving size, and nutritional level desires. By segmenting its target market and tailoring solutions to each segment, it can significantly increase its win rate. This has been the strategy of large branded food companies. Smaller companies may elect instead to serve a narrower market. The higher win rate can more than offset the reduction in potential market size, and open opportunities for less expensive or more effective ways to reach its target customers.

Companies with high win rates but low awareness and consideration rates, on the other hand, will find their richest opportunities in marketing communications and distribution/sales strategies. Claussen Pickles, a refrigerated pickles company, won all the taste tests but remained stuck with low sales growth. Investigation using this formula led managers to discover that shoppers made their pickle brand decision before they arrived at the refrigerated shelves where the company's offering was located. Pickles are among the most impulsive grocery store purchases. People bought pickles in the dried goods aisles, thereby leading them to not look for or purchase additional pickles once they hit the refrigerated shelves.

Others will discover that their market is very slow growing, demanding an expansion of the company's offering to its current target markets or the addition of new target markets to grow. On occasion, companies can also find opportunities in changing their offerings to bring more nonusers into their market. Yamaha piano did just that by transforming the piano from a musical instrument alone to an entertainment center by bringing player pianos back onto the market.

LOOK TO THE FUTURE

The sales equation can also be used to help you explore new ways to grow your revenue. Consider the following options and see which you are already doing and where you may have new ones:

- Increasing served markets (extending your products or services to new markets)

- Growing the overall market by creating offerings or channels that bring new people into the market; this strategy is a terrific one for escaping commodity competition because, as the first entrant, you are without competition

- Increasing awareness of your offering through better marketing communication tactics

- Getting considered more often by closing the product or service gaps that lead customers to stop buying from you or even considering your offering in the first place

- Increasing your win rate by creating clearer, more effective points of differentiation or better communicating them

- Selling more units per customer by finding new situations or occasions for your customers to purchase from you

- Earning a higher price by adding capabilities/features and creating advantages that eliminate some or all of the competition and lead people to pay more for your offering

Other companies find that they can grow sales by identifying the situations in which end users choose a different company's products. Line extensions enable the company to be considered for these situations. Still others increase revenue per customer by broadening their offering to current customers. Identifying other products or services used alongside your own is a rich dig site for potential additions to your company's offerings.

2. Do we or could we have a unique competency that benefits a group of customers?

This question is designed to help you document risks and opportunities related to core competencies. What is your actual or potential core competency?[6] How can you best exploit it? Where are competitors catching up, causing you to lose an existing core competency? What companies outside your industry have a core competency that would enable them to enter your industry?

Although all the components of a strategic assessment are important, the analysis of core competencies provides the catalyst for revealing true differentiation opportunities. A core competency is a vital means for creating the competitive advantage in existing and new markets that is at the heart of earning price premiums and building a thriving business.

A competency is a collection of skills and knowledge that creates an overall organizational capability. A competency describes what the company does exceptionally well through the accumulated learning of the organization and how people work together. A competency is deemed to be a *core* competency if it passes four tests (see also Table 3.1):

1. It creates customer perceived value.
2. It is difficult to replicate by a competitor.
3. It is extendable—you can build on it to help your company succeed in new markets.
4. It is clearly superior to what competitors can do.

Miniaturization (Sony), exceptional service levels at every interface (Ritz Carlton), elegant design that adds functionality (Apple), and distribution efficiency (Wal-Mart) are but four examples of core competencies.

Strategists Prahalad and Hamel, in writing about core competencies, state:

> Core competencies are the wellspring of new business development. They should constitute the focus for strategy at the corporate level. Managers have to win manufacturing leadership in core products and capture global share through brand-building programs aimed at exploiting economies of scope. Only if the company is conceived of as a hierarchy of core competencies, core products, and market-focused business units will it be fit to fight.[7]

TABLE 3.1 *Core competency*

WHAT IT IS	WHAT IT IS NOT
▪ A bundle of (depreciable) skills and technologies that generate superior value and that is reliant on cumulative learning and culture of the organization ▪ What a group does exceptionally well, defined very specifically	▪ An attribute of a material or technology ▪ An asset ▪ An individual ▪ A market requirement ▪ That which your company does for its revenue ▪ A capability with no impact on customer benefits or costs ▪ How you conduct a process or set of processes*
WHAT IT PROVIDES	**RISK IF LOST**
▪ Greater benefits or lower costs for customers ▪ Competitive advantage and victories	▪ Fighting margin battles from now until the company goes out of business

*Lots of companies have the same processes as your company. A core competency emerges in *how* you conduct your processes or *how* the different processes in your company are linked together to create customer value.

The Case for Core Competencies

The authors raise a number of reasons to care about your company's core competency, whether you have one or a few:

- Assessing competitors' current products may fool you into complacency about your current position—a company with a strong core competency will have better products tomorrow.

- A core competency helps you decide on a competitive strategy—it is what creates your differentiation and points to customer segments that would most benefit from it.

- A core competency lets you see new opportunities you wouldn't otherwise see.

- Managing a core competency ensures that your value stays superior.

- A core competency is a source of competitive advantage.

- With a core competency, customers want what you offer, and competitors can't easily replicate it.

- A core competency keeps you competitive even if unexpected entrants come into your market; it will cause other companies to not enter your market(s).

Risks of Not Having or Losing a Core Competency

If the foregoing list has not convinced you to invest the time to think hard about what your core competencies are and then work to strengthen them or create one, consider these risks of ignoring core competencies:

- Competitors may surprise you.
- You may unknowingly divest yourself of hard-to-replicate, valuable skills.
- New entrants may surprise you.
- You will limit your growth opportunities.
- You may become too dependent on your suppliers.
- You may lose key staff by not offering competitive salary and benefit packages, or by eliminating their jobs during downturns or mergers and acquisitions.
- Your market position may remain fragmented or weakened.
- Other companies may develop and overtake one of your core competencies.

Anchoring Value-Creation Strategies

Here is one last argument. Core competencies become the anchor of the value-creation strategies we will talk about in the next step because they create strategic alternatives for your company.

- They can be used to strengthen your competitive position in the markets you currently serve.
- They can be used to broaden or change your served market.
- They can be used to diversify your offering or target markets.

- You can survive without a core competency, but you will never truly thrive.

Identifying Core Competencies

With your strategic assessment team, or ideally with a still broader group that includes lower-level coworkers, answer the following questions:

- When we are at our very best, what are we doing for our customers and others? What skills, knowledge, technologies, and assets enable us to provide this value?

- What can we do that other companies cannot do?

- Which of our people or teams would be most difficult to replace, and why?

- Why do customers pay us an amount that exceeds the material, labor, and overhead costs of our products and services? What, if anything, would let us earn a price premium over the competition or a profit margin that exceeds the cost of capital?

- What have our competitors tried to copy that has proven unsuccessful? What have we done far better than our competition?

- In what areas or on what activities do the different functional areas or departments work most cooperatively? Effectively? When they work together, what are they trying to optimize? What are the hard problems they excel at solving?

- If employees from other companies came into our company for a week to replace all of us, what couldn't they do that we can do because we've been here? What activities in our company have the longest learning curves?

- Why do customers stick with us?

- Why do we attract new customers?

Now, look at the answers to these questions and search for the concepts that cut through the answers. What skills, knowledge, ways of working are behind your success and your customers' repeat orders or loyalty? How do these threads weave together? What is it that your organization does (better than other companies) that is of value to customers, that is hard to duplicate, and that can be used to move into new offerings or markets?

Be careful to not answer this question with a description that other companies could use to describe what they do. For example, every seller of roasted coffee beans roasts beans. Ancora Roasters, an independent vertically integrated coffee roaster and local chain of coffee shops, has a core competency in getting fresher beans to its own coffee shops and other independent coffee shops that it sells beans to. This creates better taste and longer coffee bean shelf life and can be used to help Ancora gain share in its own markets and move into new geographic markets. Competitor Starbucks' size and distribution complexity make it unable to compete with Ancora Roasters' richness of coffee taste.

Once you have an idea about your current or potential competency, ask:

- What target market would most benefit from this core competency?
- How can we be sure we package this competency into an offering and do not give it away for free as part of our selling process, as many manufacturers of custom products and business service firms do?
- What new offerings or markets could we move into and have an advantage in because of this core competency?
- What can we do that our competitors can't do in terms of growth opportunities?
- What benefits or cost savings can we promise and be sure to deliver to our customers because we have or could develop this core competency?
- What must we change internally to create or strengthen this core competency and make sure our competition cannot easily match our competency?

3. What factors drive our profitability?

This question is designed to help you understand what currently drives your profitability engine and the risks and opportunities related to your business model.

As part of the strategic assessment, it is important to conduct a financial analysis that enables you to identify the key drivers of your profitability. Doing things the way you are now may keep the company afloat, but will it ever lead to true long-term profitability?

WHAT IF YOU DO NOT HAVE A CORE COMPETENCY?

Knowing that your company lacks a core competency is far better than assuming you have one when you do not. When performing a strategic assessment, it is essential to think in terms of what *could emerge* as a core competency for your organization. From this perspective, you can examine the existing skills and talents of the organization and ask, "What must we do differently? What skills must we add? How can we build on what we already do well to form a core competency?"

The first way to tackle this question is to identify the customer segments, situations when they buy, the distribution channels, the locations, times of the year, and the products or services that are most profitable or have the potential to be the most profitable. You need to be Sherlock Holmes asking questions of your financial database and piecing together the clues. Highly profitable parts of your business are the least commodity-like in your portfolio. Finding the combination of factors (above) that produces your highest profit margins will identify the parts of your business that are the most differentiated and have the best growth opportunities.

With this work done, you can then ask, "What is different about these customer segments or products or services such that they contribute more to profitability than the others?" In answering this question, you will find what drives your financial success. Walgreens, for example, looking across its multiple stores and categories, discovered that the key to profitability was growing sales per customer far more than its customers per store. This became the linchpin of its strategy to be the store where you can find far more of what you need today, quickly, than mere drugstore items.

Asking "What drives our profitability?" may also lead you to reconsider key elements of your marketplace exchange. For example, an engineering consulting company knew that "billable hours" drove its revenue engine. But, in discussing profitability drivers, it also came to realize it would never achieve desired profitability levels and customer service levels with a business model of billing for time. Instead of selling engineering design hours, the company elected to move into semi-customizable modular OEM products that better leveraged the company's core competencies and created a more stable revenue flow.

One question to ask as you think about financial drivers is whether a different type of revenue exchange would benefit the bottom line. For example, the addition of leasing opens up multiple new selling opportunities. Should you sell on consignment in addition to outright sales? License your technology in addition to or as an alternative to creating products containing that technology?

Jim Collins, in *Good to Great*,[8] asks readers to identify what drives their economic engine, which is a different way of defining profitability. Understanding what drives your economic engine helps you identify the one variable that, if pursued by the company and increased over time, ensures sustained cash flow and profitability.

You can also assess profitability drivers by adopting a macro view of industry dynamics. Harvard Business School's Michael Porter, a noted strategist, identifies five forces that affect profitability:

1. Competitive rivalry within an industry

2. Threat of new entrants

3. Bargaining power of customers

4. Bargaining power of suppliers

5. Threat of substitute products

How do these factors operate in your industry? At the heart of a strategically differentiated business model is a market position that minimizes these forces shaping profitability. What changes in your business model might reduce the power of one or more of these drivers?

4. Where do we compete, and what are the pros and cons of where we compete?

This question is designed to help you think through how you define the boundaries of the market in which you currently compete and what risks and opportunities that presents.

The first question to ask is, How do your customers describe you? What frame of reference do they use? What place in a customer's mind contains your brand? In which purchasing situations are you considered and in which are you not? What do potential customers see about the range of your company's offerings and whom it serves that is different from your competitors' offerings?

Although you may think of yourself as a manufacturer, service provider, or other business, customers think about your company in a far broader context. Usually, that context is built around the solution you and your competitors provide. Therefore, define the frame of reference for your offering in the customers' terms, not yours. Is your frame of reference unique or filled with many essentially equivalent competitors, from the customer's perspective? Is there a way of describing your business—as it is today or as you'd like it to be—that creates a category of one with you as the sole member?

The second question to ask is, What industry are you in? To locate your organization's product and service offerings and target markets in the context of a broadly defined industry, we recommend doing an industry map framework exercise. Far broader than a company's typical reference, this exercise serves as a catalyst for market-driven strategic discussions on the part of the leadership team. (See Table 3.2 for an example from the home furnishings industry that was created for a window treatment company that defined its industry as hard window treatments.)

The industry map is, in essence, a matrix in which the columns identify all the potential market segments that the company and its competitors (in your broadly defined industry) could choose to serve. The rows represent all the various categories of products, technologies, and services that are supplied to customers to make their end product (in B2B markets) or that are purchased by customers.

An industry map helps your strategic assessment team step back from a narrow focus on the business you are in today and identify who might enter your markets and which potential or current competitors have the most attractive array of offerings for each market segment. This will help you do the following:

- Better identify the risks and opportunities associated with the current scope of your offerings and the categories in which you participate.
- Envision your business with a narrower, broader, or more focused set of target offerings and markets.
- Better understand where future competition might emerge.

- Provide a reference framework to identify and select specific business model strategies in terms of additional target markets and product or service offerings.

TABLE 3.2 *An example of an industry map*

TYPE CHANNEL / CATEGORY	Independent and architectural firm ASID designers	Independent furniture stores	Internet and catalog companies	Window specialty stores	Specialty home products stores (e.g., paint or flooring)	Big-box and other national retailers
Custom blinds ■ Stock ■ Cut to order ■ Made to order						
Custom shades ■ Stock ■ Sewn to order ■ Custom						
Soft curtain & drapes ■ Stock ■ Sewn to order ■ Custom						
Installation services						
Bedding ■ Stock ■ Custom						
Furniture						
Flooring						
Other home categories						

Creating an Industry Map

The secret of getting a good industry map is to *not* limit your definition of your *industry* based on your current product or service offerings. The broader definition of industry will yield more unique market insights. For example, a hair care products company would define its industry as "all beauty products" rather than "hair care products." Once you have your broad industry definition in mind, construct the industry map.

Typically, an organization will work with two, possibly three, different versions of the industry map columns in making its strategic decisions. Each map will define the industry and segment the customers of that industry in a different way. In all cases, you'll segment the total market into groups whose needs are distinctly different. For example, you could segment the construction industry markets in these categories:

- Type of buildings
- Size of projects
- Location of projects
- Type of clients

In the case of the window treatment company, it might look at one industry map by type of end user, and then a second industry map by type of store where the end user purchases the product, and a third by type of room. The segmentations of the target markets (the columns) should relate to customers having different needs and ways of being served.

With the rows and columns of the industry map(s) constructed, physically identify the squares where your company, your competitors, and companies that might enter your market do business—in other words, in what squares of the industry map matrix do they compete? Ask the following questions:

- What are the strengths and weaknesses of where we compete? For example, if you are a niche company (you have a very narrow offering to a very narrow target market), your strength is likely to be your specialized focus. Your weakness is that other companies can offer a broader and easier solution to customers—they have manufacturing or advertising economies of scale you lack or a direct sales force you cannot afford. Who could absorb your product or service niche as a standard component in their offering, pushing you further down the food chain from the ultimate end user? What additions to your offering would let you move up the food chain?

- Who might enter your market space, and what would be the risks if they did?

- Where might you grow—into what spaces on the industry map, and are these good opportunities? (A dental products company, for example, could enter the dental surgery and orthodontics market, or a company serving primarily the big-box stores might create a different set of offerings to serve the independent stores.)

- Think about the opportunities each potential target market offers by asking:

   - What are the current and unmet needs of the different target market segments, and which can we best serve over the long term?
   - Which target markets offer the most attractive growth opportunities for our company?
   - To which target markets should we not sell?

QUESTIONS TO HELP YOU CREATE YOUR OWN INDUSTRY MAP

Customer groups

- Who are the different purchasers of your products and services (position, type of company, type of use)?

- How do you divide customers in your mind? What makes them the same or different in terms of how they rate the suppliers that serve them?

- Are there different roles or functions your products serve for different customers, or different situations that the customer may face, such that their needs from the products or services are different? Window blinds for the living room and dining room serve a different set of needs than those for a bedroom, for example. Concrete serves a strictly functional role in foundations, compared to concrete for patios, garden walls, commercial building architectural precast panels, or kitchen and bathroom countertops where appearance and design elements become more important.

- What are the types of companies for whom your products and services work well, and why? For whom do your products and services not work well, and why? Are there types of customers or dealers or retail outlets you tell your sales representatives to call? Are there types you tell your representatives to not bother to call? If you could describe the ideal target customer for your organization, who would it be?

- Why would someone be using a company like yours rather than doing the work internally?

Product/service listing

- What are the substitutes for your products and services?

- What function do your products and services perform in your customers' organizations?

- What would you call the industry that includes your products and services?

- What are the services you've actually offered or could potentially offer associated with bringing your products to a customer? (You might want to think through your most complicated sale.)

- Are there any services or products your competitors offer that you do not?

- What are the complementary products that go along with your core product line—not necessarily those you offer but that your customers would acquire from other companies?

- Are there any services or products you offer that have not been identified here?

Competitors

- What are the different types of companies with whom you compete? (You may want to group them according to the scope of their products and services, how they compete, their size, or other elements that differentiate one group from another.)

- Are there any products and services these competitors offer that have not been identified here?

5. Are we currently strategically differentiated from our competition?

This question is designed to help you understand how and what your current and potential customers think about your business and, again, what risks and opportunities that presents.

This question, more than any other, requires ruthless honesty on the part of your team. By addressing it, you establish the current strategic positioning of your firm and that of your current or potential competitors, which could pose the greatest risks going forward.

The strategic business model components for your company or business unit are

- Target market(s) served
- Frame of reference in the customer's mind for offering or scope of your business
- Value proposition—why your company's offering is selected over that of the competition
- Evidence that your company can deliver on this value proposition

Once you have compiled the answers, see if you pass the following test of whether or not your business is strategically differentiated:

- Customers clearly see the distinction between you and your competition.
- Customers value this distinction.
- You have shifted from bid to negotiation, or from limited shelf space to more shelf space, or from winning on price[9] to winning on unique benefits or compelling cost savings other than reduced purchase price.
- You have loyal customers for reasons other than too much demand chasing too little supply.
- Your margins are high and attractive, especially versus the competition.
- Your areas of differentiation endure from year to year versus being driven by fiscal year imperatives.
- Other companies face too many hurdles to try to copy one or more of your elements of differentiation, or will fail in trying.

If these are true, then your company's business model is strategically differentiated. If these conditions are not true, then use the answers about what customers value and what they struggle with to help you start carving out a business model that *will* be differentiated.

If your company's overall offering is not differentiated, discuss whether any specific product or service might be differentiated or if there is any niche group of customers where you are differentiated. If so, what is the differentiation, and why does it matter to customers? This examination will yield insights into growth opportunities and unique positions you might hold in a broader market. Discuss if there is a potential way to differentiate the whole of your offering in the eyes of your target market. If not, is there a target market where you could hold a differentiated position because it is not well served today?

CREATE A BUSINESS MODEL FOR
THE WHOLE COMPANY OR BUSINESS UNIT

It may be very hard to define your strategic differentiation or business model for the entire business. You may be drawn to want to do this work by product category within the business unit. Try not to go down this path. Remember that the work we are doing is positioning the entire company's offerings—so as to build value behind the whole of the offering. It is important to uncover the danger of having an individual product or category that is differentiated, while the overall offering is not. Compel your leaders to think about how they might be able to add value to their overall offering by thinking about a different business model. Kraft's brands increasingly compete against their niche competitors (e.g., Hormel versus Kraft's Oscar Mayer), as well as store brands and other large food product companies. What can Kraft (or its business unit containing Oscar Mayer brand products) offer that would add value across all its category offerings so that the brand name adds compelling advantages to all its consumer offerings? The work of differentiating one specific product or narrow category and brand for the multiple brand company or business unit will come later, as marketing managers work within the context of the strategically differentiated business model.

6. What sacrifices and compromises must customers make to use our industry's offerings that we might be able to help them avoid?

You are most vulnerable to competition in areas where your customers are unhappy, even if they currently accept their struggles and compromises as simply part of doing business with your industry. This question will help you uncover customer sacrifices and the risks and opportunities they present.

Every industry develops basic rules about how it creates and delivers its offerings to target markets. These rules inevitably create compromises—issues that arise for customers because suppliers have elected to trade off one internal benefit for another.

To identify compromises, you must discover customers' unmet needs and key strategic issues. The list of proposed questions for customers (page 91, following the discussion of the ten core strategic assessment questions) includes asking customers about compromises they feel they must make when dealing with your industry. Typically, this is not the subject matter of conversations between customers and suppliers, as customers take these trade-offs as a given.

A common compromise that innovative companies have capitalized upon is an industry offering that is overbuilt and therefore too costly for many. A scaled-down offering will create a strong position with some existing industry customers and bring still others into the market. Micro-lending is an example of this type of disruption in global financial markets.

Examine the feedback from the interviews or focus groups you engaged in prior to doing the strategic assessment. Your task now is to identify which of these issues you can do something about. Look at your company's potential core competencies. Can they be used to address any of these compromises or trade-offs? Are there any new offerings (ideally new to market) that would address any of these trade-offs?

Matching your company's knowledge with a deeper understanding of customer issues, compromises, frustrations, and opportunities results in ideas for new services, product offerings, and features. You know you've addressed a customer compromise when you find yourself with a product, service, or competitive edge that competitors can't match. You know you have strategic differentiation when your customers are telling you, "Wow! How did we *ever* get by without this?"

7. What are the strong and weak positions in our current offerings and markets?

This question will help you identify risks and opportunities related to the configuration of your current portfolio.

Some organizations have multiple products, multiple categories, multiple target markets, or multiple businesses under one roof. Understanding the competitive position and the market conditions surrounding each can reveal deeper insights regarding your business.

We recommend using matrices to facilitate answering questions about your portfolio. In one typical matrix (see Table 3.3), the *rows* refer to the position of your company versus the competition in each of its offerings:

- Dominant or very strong—share far outweighs that of the competition.
- Favorable—high share, but there is close competition.
- Tentative—weakest of the companies participating actively in this market.
- Weak—not really a player, or a threat, in competitors' opinion.

The *columns* of the matrix refer to market conditions for the offering and its competitive alternatives:

- Early adoption—the market is just starting to emerge.
- Growth—significant year-to-year sales gains.

TABLE 3.3 *What are the strong and weak positions in your portfolio?*

Our Position \\ Market	Early Adoption	Growth	Stable	Decline
Dominant/Very Strong				
Favorable				
Tentative				
Weak				

- Stable—growth is leveling off.
- Decline—size is declining as substitutes take more market share.

You may also choose to use market size growth (below average, average, and higher than average), operating margin (low, average, high versus your overall operating margin), or market attractiveness (a combination of market growth and competitive intensity) to divide the columns.

Using this matrix, you can evaluate where each of your categories and target markets (or business units if you have multiple business units) stand in terms of the market and life cycle by placing each in the appropriate intersection of columns and rows. If you find too many weak or unattractive positions, be sure to factor that into your risks and opportunities. You will also be able to identify which offerings are least commodity-like (based on margins) and whether there are ways to begin to define a strategically differentiated business model around these types of offerings.

8. Is the whole of our business worth more than its individual parts?

This question will help you identify potential synergies that may present good opportunities for your business and overcome risks previously identified.

Synergies exist when the success of the total offering or target markets served exceeds how successful the company would be if it did not serve as broad a group or have as broad an offering. For example, when serving multiple market segments provides economies of scale to a company, we view these market segments as synergistic. Or, when a broader product offering creates valued time-savings for customers, we view these products to be synergistic.

Visible signs of synergies in different industries include the following:

- P&G has a broad offering of products that lets it leverage its marketing and selling resources and build an umbrella brand name over individual product brand names.
- Apple captures synergies between different computing hardware components and software by offering products that excel in design and ease of use but also work very easily with one another, saving customers time and avoiding frustrations.

- UPS entered the packaged travel flight business by employing planes during times other than when it is engaged in package delivery.
- National chain retail stores, such as Wal-Mart, are capturing buying, distribution, and marketing synergies across geographic locations.

Manufacturing costs can also be a source of synergies. But be very wary of *overhead absorption* arguments. The assumption that serving multiple markets, and creating a broader array of products across which to absorb overhead costs, will lower overall costs for any one product line is not necessarily valid. Often, the breadth of such offerings creates complexity that only *adds* to overhead costs.

Other potential sources of synergy include the following: sales, marketing, and large administrative costs; management and market knowledge; consideration factors; sales representative effectiveness and costs; product bundling; and integration and leverage of assets. Be very wary of claiming cost synergies that reduce business effectiveness. For example, many companies create a shared sales force to capture selling synergies across multiple business units. In the process, units that need a different type of selling may be shortchanged. Or, the addition of "specialists" within a consolidated sales force to manage different needs of business units may create a level of complexity. Finally, there may not be sufficient financial incentives for the shared sales force to secure a leading market position for some of the business units despite having better products and services than their competition. In addition to identifying existing synergies, be sure to discuss these questions:

- What is not synergistic, and should we participate in these market segments?
- What could we add to our offering or what target markets could we add that would be most synergistic with our existing business?

Synergistic growth is profitable growth and that, after all, is what you are after through growth—profits, not revenue for the sake of revenue alone.

9. What is the larger value chain of which we are a part, and is the overall value chain well designed to deliver maximum value to target groups of customers?

This question is designed to help you determine whether there are opportunities to reconfigure your value chain—adding or eliminating steps inside your business—and what risks may accrue if you don't do so.

This question can be answered by performing a value chain analysis focused on the unique aspects of your industry. A value chain is a visual representation of all the companies and key steps for transforming raw inputs into a product or service used by the end user (see Figure 3.1). A gourmet restaurant's value chain would identify the independent companies from which it gets its ingredients and the key steps in which it engages to serve its customers' meals. A fast-food franchise restaurant's value chain, by contrast, would identify that its ingredients come from the franchiser. And wait staff would not be a part of the value chain, whereas it would be for the gourmet restaurant.

To create your company's value chain, work backward to understand where your purchased materials and services come from. Then work forward to identify where the product goes after it leaves your company and before it gets to the end user. (Some companies may have a direct-to-consumer business, such as Pleasant Company's direct mail catalog and Nike's retail stores.)

A value chain analysis evaluates whether all the participants and activities leading to the production and distribution of the end-user product or service is well designed. You discover strategic insights by asking questions like: "How could we reconfigure our business to combine or eliminate different steps of the value chain? How can we manage our relationship to suppliers and customers to reduce costs or increase end-user benefits—and ultimately increase value?" The large big-box office stores are examples of companies that concluded, "We can end our reliance on small, independent office supplies companies to reach customers." By eliminating the distribution step and opening large retail centers in their place, Office Depot and Staples reinvented the office products industry.

In conducting the strategic assessment, you can evaluate where you fit in the value chain and develop a strategy to improve your overall competitive position in the value chain and the ability of the total value chain to meet customers' needs and wants.

VALUE CHAIN

TAKING OUT STEPS ENHANCED VALUE TO OWNERS AND CREATED
A WINNING, UNIQUE BUSINESS MODEL FOR FINFROCK D-M-C

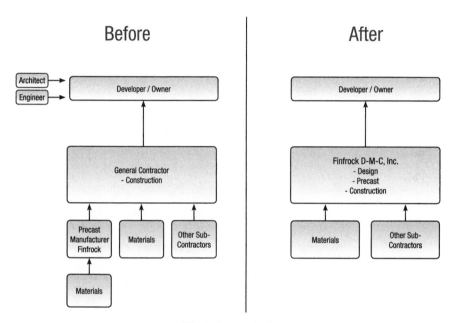

FIGURE 3.1 *The before and after value chain*

10. What is changing externally, and how will that affect our orthodoxies about our markets and our business?

By helping you to understand the marketplace and your competitors, this question will help you identify whether market forces are presenting your business with new risks or opportunities.

Companies already in a leadership position are likely to stay in that position unless they become complacent and stop listening to customers or watching competitors. However, a *changing* market ultimately brings all players back to a level playing field. This creates an opportunity for companies strategically positioned to win market share in a changing market.

Start by identifying what is changing in your market space—such as customer demand levels, buying process, buying influence, and buying criteria. Include technical, social, regulatory, and economic changes. Competitors, complementary product companies, and industry supplier changes are also important, as are changes in the labor force.

External changes destroy the existing market paradigms or customary beliefs around which businesses built their competitive advantage. The companies that are first to anticipate how change will impact their industry, and then act on this insight, are able to exploit change to their advantage. For example, there are significant differences between baby boomers and the new generation X and Y workers. The companies that understand this and made early changes in their work environments (e.g., to introduce flextime and to move jobs to where young people want to live) have been winning the war for talent. Other baby boomer–led companies, that still think every worker should behave the way the baby-boom generation did, have outdated work policies. With the retirement of the baby boomers, strategically positioning your company to attract and retain talent (and not just customers) will become increasingly important.

In addition to looking at what is changing, identify the paradigms and customary beliefs that people in your leadership team, company, or even industry hold about how business works in your markets and industry. As shown in the Finfrock story from the introduction, for example, the old standard orthodoxy in the precast industry was that the general contractor was the customer of the precast subcontractor. The owner hired the general contractor, who then hired all the subcontractors and oversaw construction of the building. Finfrock had to break this paradigm in order to break out of its commodity box.

It's important to recognize that changes occur when there are opposing forces at work. Thus, in looking at what is changing, you should try to identify *turning points* and *breakpoints*.[10]

- *Turning points are trends that create their own backlash.* For example, consolidation in the publishing industry for K-12 schoolbooks created a lot of me-too programs and offerings that teachers felt compromised classroom education. In wave after wave of consolidation, new niche start-ups and entrants into the K-12 school publishing market (e.g., Scholastic) emerged with fresh ideas and creative offerings that won teachers over. Turning points show up in every industry.

- *Breakpoints occur when two trends are diametrically opposed, or where one trend is offset by very strong resistance from a second trend.* For example, there is a growing need for cost containment in health care because the price of health care is causing many employers to stop offering benefits and others to push more costs to employees. New buying approaches are being introduced to try to drive down the cost of health care. But as baby boomers age, greater demand for health care services will drive prices up. These two opposing trends—one driving prices up and one driving them down—are likely to create a breakpoint in the health care market.

Turning points are trends that predictably and gradually change directions: more of something followed by less of it. Watching the trend, one can more easily anticipate when it will reach its peak and reverse course. Demographic changes, for example, will create known and therefore easily anticipated turning points. Breakpoints, by contrast, arise suddenly and unexpectedly, creating changes no one might have anticipated before their arrival. If the baby boomers face a Medicare health program lacking today's benefit levels, there may be a huge rush of retirees seeking part-time work with benefits, a genuine opportunity for a national staffing firm like Manpower. Companies that can anticipate breakpoints in their market trends will have a leg up over the competition.

As you look at all that is changing and your orthodoxies, identify the following:

- Known trends and their implications for your company, given your current orthodoxies. What risks or opportunities are created if you change your orthodoxy? If you do not change it?

- Potentially emerging trends and their implications for your company, given your current orthodoxies. What risks or opportunities are created if you change your orthodoxy?

- Trends in opposition to current ways of doing business that may create a breakpoint. How could your company exploit or bring about a breakpoint?

Getting Answers to the Ten Questions: Developing a Strategic Assessment Plan

Every company has a unique history and structure that defines a set of unique challenges both internally and in the marketplace. Therefore, we can't present a simple boilerplate plan for getting the information you need. Instead, we'll present some tips and guidelines about external information gathering to help you develop your own plan.

What follows is a list of information sources people can turn to and what they can gather from each source. Review the guidelines and compare the answers you'd expect to get from each source to the previous ten questions. If a source doesn't help you with *any* of the questions, then it is probably irrelevant to your exploration plan and can be skipped. If none of these sources helps you answer a question, you'll have to think outside your own box to develop an innovative way to get the information you need. There are five issues you need to think through:

1. Typical sources of information
   - Existing
   - Information from outside resources

2. What you need to do to understand customers and end users
   - Questions to ask
   - How many, and which customers to ask questions of

3. What you can learn from your key suppliers, distribution channel partners, and complementary product companies

4. What you can learn from experts

5. Putting the pieces together into a coherent plan

Let's walk through each of these areas.

What are typical sources of information?

Existing Information

- Past proprietary market research reports.

- Multiclient market research reports. However, these reports rarely provide information specific enough to your business to be relied on as the only information you use to make your assessment.

- Other published material pertinent to your industry, customer base, and technology, gathered from publications, the Web, seminars, and so on. For example, the publications that your customers and their customers read are especially helpful for identifying trends and issues facing your customer base.

- Competitors' Web sites, press releases, media references, and, if the company is publicly traded, annual and quarterly reports and stock analyst reports.

- Web sites of companies selling complementary products and services (used alongside your own).

- Your company's financial statements—overall, by business unit, by product category, by market, by channel, and in B2B markets, by customer. Prepare your finance department to create new cross-tabulations of financial information against these views of the data as well.

- Any tracking information on market size, market share, penetration rates (percentage of the market that has ever considered you or used you), repeat purchase rates, win rates (once considered), and any other variable that measures outcome of your selling process.

Information You Can Collect from Outside Resources

However you choose to gather information, it is critical that it come from the right people. The exact list of outside resources will clearly depend on your company and industry and the amount you can invest in information collection. The point is that the absence of new outside information in your strategic assessment process will severely limit its potential to surface actionable strategic insights. Work with a market research expert to identify the best methodology to gather information. In B2B markets, one-on-one interviews are typically the best way to gather information. Although quantitative information is helpful, qualitative information can be less costly to collect (as you need fewer interviews) and far richer in terms of insights. Qualitative research (focus group, phone or personal interviews) is often conducted by a more experienced questioner who can, in the moment, ask probing questions that are at the heart of new insights. Examples of vital sources of qualitative information include the following:

- Current, lost, and potential customers are all valuable sources of insight into your company—insights that will deepen your understanding of your company's risks and opportunities.

- Potential customer groups not using your industry's offerings because they are either too feature laden and expensive or lacking in needed features will offer insights into potential market growth opportunities.

- End users of your industry's offering (including those who chose a competitor) are also a rich source of insights into strategic risks and opportunities.

- Key suppliers are often familiar with your competition.

- Companies selling complementary offerings can be useful sources of information.

- Experts in any area (e.g., technology, societal factors, etc.) that will impact your market are potential sources of information.

What do you need to do to understand customers?

Getting information from and about customers is a multifaceted venture. Yes, you'll want to conduct interviews (and we have some tips here), but you can't rely on what customers tell you as your sole source of information about their needs, either met or unmet. For one thing, you can be sure that anything they *say* to you they are also saying to your competitors. You have to know for yourself what it feels like to be in your peers' position in that company or in the consumer's life. What are the things that they take for granted and do not share with you? What problems recur? What frustrations exist? What makes your customers successful? Delighted? Be attentive and try to understand their daily frustrations with their jobs or lives and with your industry and offering. Listen for messages related to *their* strategic direction and success factors or deepest held values and emotional needs.

That's why one of the best ways to discover customer compromises is to walk a mile in their shoes. You must understand exactly what it feels like to be running a customer's business or living your consumer's life. You must obtain a clear understanding of the compromises they face as well as an appreciation of the sacrifices they make on a repetitive basis, not just with your industry but with everything they touch. New anthropological market research techniques, such as watching your customers use your product, allow companies to accomplish just this. Quaker Oats learns of parents' frustration with unhealthy quick breakfast and snack foods and expands its offerings to include oats-based breakfast and snack bars.

Another way to unearth actionable target market insights is to identify jobs the customers are getting done by themselves or with another industry with which the customer is highly dissatisfied. Expanding your offering to incorporate these jobs can be a great way to innovate your offering. For example, the balloons used to open up arteries in angioplasty procedures and thereby prevent heart attacks are also being used today to deliver a stent to the artery to ensure that it remains open. Prior to this innovation, medication was used to prevent the need for additional angioplasty, but with weak overall results. Observing the customer using your offering or competitors' offerings is also a way of identifying the frustrations and compromises your customers have with your industry.

Questions for Customers

There are specific questions you need to ask customers to get a realistic perspective on why they selected you or why you lost or never earned their business. This will go a long way toward understanding, and ultimately improving, your differentiation.

You will want to learn about the following factors from customers (business or consumers) who buy your offering. Ask them questions such as:

- What most frustrates you in your job (B2B markets) or life (business-to-consumer [B2C] markets)? What defines success and well-being for you?

- What core issues are you trying to tackle?

- What one change would fundamentally alter, in a positive fashion, your business success or personal well-being?

- Are there different situations you face when using our industry products that lead you to purchase from different companies rather than only one company? What are they?

- What do you expect from a company to even consider purchasing from it?

- Which factors are most important in deciding which alternative you choose?

- Why don't you self-perform what you are purchasing from the outside?

- What work do you wish companies would take over from you?

- What factors create loyalty or a defined preference for one company over another?

- What factors create conditions for giving more volume to one company over another?

- What factors differentiate competitors and typically affect the decisions about who wins and loses?

- (If current or past customer) What feelings do you have when you think about or use our products or services?

- Why do you buy (not buy or stopped buying, depending on your status with the customer) our products?

- What do you see our company doing well? Where is improvement needed?

- What, if anything, differentiates our company from our competitors?

- What could you see us doing to better serve you and grow our business with you and others like you?

- What about our industry frustrates you? What compromises do you need to make to work with suppliers in our industry?

- What product categories or companies outside our industry work really well from your perspective in meeting your needs? Can you provide one or two examples?

BE SURE TO CONTACT DISTRIBUTORS, MANUFACTURERS REPRESENTATIVE ORGANIZATIONS, RETAILERS, OR OTHER CHANNEL PARTNERS

Ask them the following questions about your product:

- What is your image of our company/brand? How would you describe us to others?
- What company do you see as most equivalent to us? Why that company?
- If you ran our company, what changes would you make?
- What most frustrates you about our product or service category—irrespective of the specific supplier? What do you wish all the companies in this category would do differently to make your experience better and your life better?
- What jobs would you like someone to take over from you?

The most important insights gained through this process are sometimes not the information contained in the direct answers to questions but a better understanding of your customers' businesses and their customers. This knowledge can help you determine how you may best differentiate your offering to become a truly valued supplier/brand.

How Many and Which Customers to Ask Questions Of

A common question leaders ask is, "How many customers, lost customers, and potential customers should we interview?" There is a vital need for quantitative research to track market share, market size, and customer satisfaction, and this information should be brought into the strategic assessment. The type of new interviews done for strategic assessment work ideally should be qualitative (one-on-one interviews or focus groups). More open-ended questions will provide richer insights. Also, do not use sales representatives in the interview process with B2B customers, other than to make an initial introduction. Salespeople listen for what will sell today, and customers are often not straightforward with salespeople, as they need to preserve an ongoing relationship. Furthermore, they always want to emphasize to sales personnel that price counts. Finally, be sure you interview more than the purchasing department when interviewing a business. The richest insights will come from other departments in your customers' businesses and from their senior leaders.

YOU MAY WANT TO USE OUTSIDE RESEARCHERS FOR SOME CUSTOMER CONTACT

Sometimes people inside your company can complete the research work related to answering the questions. However, especially when customers are hesitant to open up directly to you, it's best to use an outside researcher. For example, in B2B markets you are likely to get better information when you use an outside researcher to identify why you were never considered or lost business. In B2C markets an extensive array of experts and services exists to capture the voice of the customer. Even when customers are very easy to reach and direct in their assessment, it is still preferable to use an outside researcher because some managers hear only what they want to hear. Also, talented outside experts offer fresh interpretations and strategic insights that you may miss owing to company and industry paradigms.

What can you learn from suppliers and complementary products companies?

Here, your goal is to see how these sources view your industry:

- How do you divide companies in our industry—are there types that are clearly different from each other? Where do we fit?

- How do you segment our industry's customers—are there types that need different things from us versus our competitors? What are they, and how are they different?

- How would you describe us to others? Would you recommend us? For what type of customer/situation? When would we not be a good fit?

- What are our strengths and weaknesses? Are we unique in any way?

- What trends are shaping your industry? Your customers?

- What are the key challenges facing your industry? What are the key external uncertainties that companies in your industry face that will significantly impact your future and that of your industry?

- What one change in your mind would fundamentally improve our company? Our industry?

What you can learn from experts

Here, the questions will be very tailored to the expert. Ask questions that establish how the expert sees the world changing and its potential ramifications for your customers and your industry. Be sure to find out what the known trends and changes are, versus uncertain trends. How quickly are trends creating change?

Pulling the pieces together: How can you create a coherent plan?

Once you've reviewed the various sources and identified which you need to use for your assessment, you'll need to make decisions about who does the research and who will they interview, what questions you will ask, when you'll do the work, where the conversations will occur, and how you'll gather input, be it one-on-one interviews or a focus group or observing customers using your products before you ask them more probing questions. The actual work is typically carried out by either individual members or subsets of the larger assessment team, followed by a "pull it together" session where results are shared and compiled.

As you embark on this journey, make sure you document anything you hear or read that relates to a risk and opportunity for your business. Capture notes related to both target markets and points of differentiation. This information will form the basis of your analysis in the next step. Keep the tracking format simple (see Table 3.4).

Remember, this is an information-gathering step. In Step 4, we'll show you what to do with all the information on risks and opportunities that you've gathered.

TABLE 3.4 *Tracking form*

STRATEGIC ASSESSMENT QUESTION	RISKS	OPPORTUNITIES	OTHER NOTES
1. Why sales are what they are			
2. Current or potential core competencies			
3. Profitability drivers			
4. Pros and cons of where we compete			
5. Are we strategically differentiated?			
6. Customer or end-user/consumer compromises and frustrations in dealing with industry offerings			
7. Strong and weak positions in current portfolio			
8. Synergies			
9. Value chain design			
10. External changes			

Do your homework in detail. Adopt the mind-set of someone who is a newcomer to your business and industry. To develop a new understanding of how to provide value to your customers, you have to be genuinely innovative, creating an overall offering that is prized by your customers but costs you less to produce than it's worth in the customers' eyes.

Leading Your Team through the Assessment

Take our word for it, you're going to encounter a lot of resistance and fear as you go through this assessment. Why? Because facing reality is one of the hardest things a leadership team can do, as it requires leaders to own up to the true risks inherent in the company's position and their own career positions. Personal fear is why so many strategic plans are really a set of wishes with no clear pathway for how the organization will realize them. Or, they grossly underestimate risks facing the business, as Sears did with Wal-Mart.

How will leaders resist engaging in this step?

Leaders often pursue one of two strategies to avoid facing reality. They may say, "Things are not so bad," or they may find fault in others' suggested changes and improvements in the business. Beware of individuals who participate in the strategic assessment who keep pulling the group down with comments like "We tried that before and it did not work," "We could never accomplish that," or "Our customers will never let us do that." There will be plenty of time in later steps to turn recommendations into reality. The purpose in this step is to understand reality and then think creatively about where you can go, not how to get there.

A more subtle form of push back comes from leaders who think the answer to the company's commodity-induced troubles comes solely from increasing productivity or marketability of current offerings. Although increasing productivity and marketability is frequently necessary, doing so will not pull you out of the grip of commodity markets and put you into thrive mode.

How do you overcome this resistance to change?

The only way to overcome push back is to make sure you have strong, diverse, nonjudgmental, and creative conceptual thinkers at the table when you do the strategic assessment.

Conclusion

A strategic assessment provides an honest assessment of your company's longer-term growth risks and opportunities. When it is done well, members of the leadership team will feel more concerned about the present if the company does not change. They'll also be more optimistic about the future if the company has the will to change and realize the opportunities surfaced in this step. Encourage your colleagues to take off their rose-colored glasses or to lay aside their pessimism in order to build enthusiasm for creating a stronger, more opportunity-filled company.

STEP 3 KEY POINTS

Become a consultant to your own business—conduct a strategic assessment to capture fresh market insights and new risks and opportunities.

Desired goals:
- ✔ Commit as a leadership team to strategically assess your business.
- ✔ Break out of operational thinking and into strategic thinking about your business.
- ✔ Capture fresh market insights that can positively transform your business.
- ✔ Identify and prioritize risks and opportunities facing your business.

Keys to success:
- ✔ Do not be defensive. The past is the past; there is no need to defend it.
- ✔ Unearth beliefs about your business that are not necessarily true.
- ✔ Bring in new people and new information from the marketplace to help discover patterns of thinking, reveal unforeseen risks, and unearth hidden opportunities.
- ✔ Conduct your strategic assessment after budgets are done, not immediately before annual budgeting.
- ✔ Remember that competition can come from places you least expect.
- ✔ Try to answer all ten questions, recognizing that some questions will bring stronger insights into your opportunities and threats than others.

Become a consultant to your own business to capture fresh market insights into new risks and opportunities.

PART II

Design the Business You Want to Run

Never leave your most important strategic questions—
where you compete and why you win—to history or serendipity.

Steps 1, 2, and 3 presented ways in which you could challenge the status quo and gather information about what's really happening with your customers and the marketplace. Part II takes you through the three steps needed to convert these insights into a viable business model.

Step 4: Design a New Strategically Differentiated Business Model.

Step 5: Realign the Leadership Team.

Step 6: Create a Meaningful Corporate Aspiration.

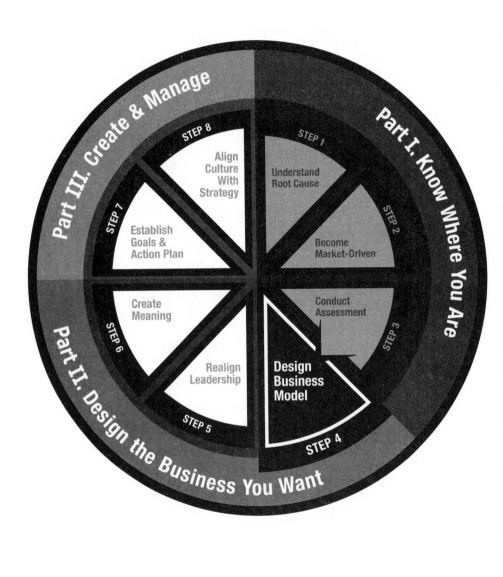

Step 4

Design a New Strategically Differentiated Business Model

The same business model will give you the same old results . . . or worse.

David's company, which he inherited from his father, manufactured fabric covers and accessory products bearing the brand name of boat and boat engine and hoist manufacturers. They also sold to manufacturers of medical equipment products, motorcycles, office equipment, lawn and garden equipment, and a host of other types of equipment manufacturers. The branded-goods companies then resold the products to their users through the manufacturers' distribution channels. David's company also sold its own branded covers for some of this equipment through the same distribution channels the equipment manufacturers used. Terrific service at competitive prices built David's business.

But being a U.S.-based commercial sewing company in the 1990s was a problem, as production was shifting overseas. David didn't want to move his company's production overseas, since it was one of the major employers in the small community in the rural northern part of his state. But prices were dropping faster than David's company could cut its costs.

David and his leadership team determined they needed to add value to the fabric accessories if they wanted to survive the onslaught of Asian imports. Service alone was not enough to differentiate their offering from lower-priced competition. "How can we leverage our service competency?" became a vitally important conversation during a strategic assessment.

Interviews with the original equipment manufacturers revealed that the fabric covers and accessory items were more a nuisance than a core part of the equipment manufacturers' businesses. The nuisance level was especially high in customers' sales forces, with sales reps frustrated with having to sell accessories that sold for under $100 alongside equipment that sold at multiples of ten times or more. Naturally, they focused on the equipment, and sales of accessory items through their distribution channels languished.

David and his team began asking and answering some tough strategic questions, like "What can we do to end customers' frustrations with our industry?" and "What business do we want to be in?" They realized there was an opportunity to take over the entire accessory business for their original equipment manufacturer (OEM) customers. Their new business model would make David's business a virtual subsidiary to the equipment manufacturers. The company would identify product needs, develop and make the products, and then merchandise them through the equipment manufacturers' distribution channels.

That led the team to ask even tougher questions about its business idea, such as, "How will we successfully convince them to switch more of their accessory business to us?" and "Can we defend ourselves against Asian competition?" The leadership team decided its business could offer the equipment manufacturers the best financial return versus the overseas competition: The equipment manufacturers would gain an attractive profit flow from their accessory business without any investment of capital or staff time. As for whether or not the new business approach would be unique, the team realized that its U.S. location now became an asset rather than a liability, as Asian manufacturers would be unable to act in a similar fashion.

David's leadership team eventually elected to narrow the focus on the marine industry, as trying to manage end-user knowledge and distribution channels in multiple markets would overwhelm the staff. The company gave up business in medical, lawn and garden, motorcycle, and other markets to gain a dominant and more profitable position in the marine market.

The new business model worked exceptionally well and even led David's company to become a favored supplier of still other fabric accessory products sold as standard items on marine equipment manufacturers' products. Furthermore, David's company was able to expand its own branded products line, leveraging the skills his company developed for the original equipment manufacturers. His company's branded products were typically purchased as replacements when the fabric accessory products carrying the marine manufacturers' brand wore out.

What David's leadership team did was take the lessons from its strategic assessment to redefine the company's business model. Rather than continue to compete in a commodity market of commercial sewing companies, the team changed the scope of the company's business and became a niche provider that not only was unparalleled in the industry but also was unique because no other competitor could offer the same benefits. And that's what being a strategically differentiated company is all about.

As David's company discovered, doing a strategic assessment was just a midpoint on its journey. It needed to interpret what the team learned and saw in order to unearth a market space where it could become, and remain, differentiated from its competition.

As discussed in the introduction, a strategically differentiated business model, executed effectively, will provide your organization with the following:

- Customers willing to pay a premium for your offering
- Longer-term relationships with customers and suppliers
- Different parts of the organization working collaboratively because they have a shared understanding of where and how you want to win business
- Easier and faster decision making related to pursuing opportunities
- Easier resolution of conflicts that naturally arise between different parts of the organization
- Better resource leveraging because the company is far more focused

Achieving this level of direction and performance depends on the outcomes of the four decisions that will define your strategically differentiated business model.

Where will you compete?

1. What is your target market, and in what situations are you its best choice?

2. What business do you want to be in?

Why will you win business?

3. What is your differentiated value promise?

4. What are your strategic advantages that allow you to deliver on this value promise in ways competitors cannot easily match?

Collectively, the answers to these questions describe the market space you are creating and defending against all existing and potential competitors.

Such key decisions cannot be left to history or serendipity. These are the most important strategic decisions a leadership team will make. Your decisions must build on the insights gained in the strategic assessment, which show you where risks exist and opportunities await. If your leadership team fails to explicitly define your organization's business model, you will be stuck in survival mode with the competition controlling your future.

In this step, we review the four strategic decisions in more detail, then show how they can help you strengthen your understanding and evaluation of the risks and opportunities identified during the assessment. That evaluation, coupled with the strategic thinking advice in this chapter, can help you define different business model options. With these options in hand, you'll make the final decision about which business model will be the best vehicle to move your company or keep your company out of commodity markets.

Identifying Four Strategic Decisions

Whether deliberate or not, every business is shaped by answering these two questions:

1. Where will you compete?

2. Why will you win business?

Responding to these questions sets up four strategic decisions, two for each question.

Where will you compete?

Where you compete is about a lot more than geography. Where you compete refers to the marketplace in which you choose to conduct business. Customers, product offering, geography, customer situation, and even technology are part of the "where you compete" strategic decisions.

There are two interrelated decisions pertaining to where your company chooses to compete.

Decision 1: What is your target market, and in what situations are you its best choice?

Most business leaders have at least a gut-level understanding of what a target market is—that is, the group(s) of businesses or consumers who they think are most likely to benefit from and hence purchase their product or service. But there's another level of detail that can be helpful—understanding the "situations" in which those target markets can benefit most. An architectural firm, for example, could have stopped at defining its target market as any company or person that wanted to have office design work done. But it pushed that definition further when it realized that it excelled when the client's project was highly complex in terms of functional, contextual, or performance (schedule and budget) dimensions. Targeting these potential client situations and designing the company around the capabilities needed to handle complex projects, rather than more easily designed projects, allowed the company to win at a far higher rate. The restaurant industry is a great one for understanding situation segmentation. Any one diner might participate in very different eating situations, choosing a different restaurant for each situation (e.g., McDonald's offers a fast food, Ruth's Chris Steak House a high-end dinner, perhaps for clients, and Applebee's an affordable family meal). Although *situation* defines customer needs, many companies do not think about it when they segment and define their target market. Choosing niche situations can be a key driver of value, growth, and differentiation.

Decision 2: What business do you want to be in?

Different businesses in the same industry serving the same target market will have different ways to define what business they are in. It is very important to define the business you are in from the target market's perspective, not your internal perspective. For David's company (from the story at the beginning of the chapter), the phrase "your subsidiary" contains far more strategic insight, communication of value, and guidance to David's people than defining their business model as "products and services to create and sell fabric accessory products."

Another important aspect of what business you are in is your revenue exchange, referred to in Step 3. Revenue exchange refers to how the customer is paying (e.g., outright sale, lease, consignment, per usage charge, per hour, maintaining equipment in use, outright sale, per project, etc.). We encourage you to think about revenue exchange as you discuss "What business are we in?" For instance, are you licensing technology or developing the final products that employ it? You may find that your value proposition can be stronger with one revenue exchange than another.

The definition of the business you are in is a huge driver of value. As shown in David's example, by redefining his business for his same target market, he moved into a monopoly position forcing competitors to play a different game or catch up.

Why will you win business?

The second major component of any business model is why you will win business over other companies. There are two components to why you win.

Decision 3: What is your differentiated value promise?

Your *differentiated value promise* is the reason customers will select your company's offerings over those of the competition. There are other words we could use for this concept that communicate the idea as well, such as unique selling proposition. However you name it, it must be defined in terms of benefits that the target market will value *or* cost and risk reductions that it will value.

You can think about the value proposition as the "legs" of the brand on your business's offerings. It is the promise the offering will be designed to fulfill.

YOU ARE HERE

Link to previous steps: The strategic assessment left the leadership team with lots of insights into the risks and opportunities facing the organization—what will happen if no changes are made and the types of changes that could fundamentally and positively transform the organization and its future. This chapter helps the leadership team apply the insights from the strategic assessment to define a new business model for the organization.

Expected outcome: Decisions on fundamental strategic issues that define what business you want to be in and why you will win market share in that market.

Who is involved: The leadership team drives the work of this step. Some companies may decide to have broader involvement, including key up and coming talent or an outside business advisor with strong strategy skills. If leaders feel uncomfortable about this work, it is best to keep the group small and then use Step Six's input-gathering stage to improve and fine-tune the business model.

Why this step is important: Once a business has fallen into commodity competition or is getting a lot closer to it, some aspect of the four anchors of the business model must change. Otherwise, you stay stuck in the process of making improvements whose value all flows to the customer, not to your bottom line.

Emotion is also an important part of the brand and value proposition, especially when it comes to merchandising and communications. Be wary of thinking so much about the emotional elements of your brand, however, that you give too little attention to the direct and indirect tangible benefits and costs that are critical to the value proposition.

Decision 4: What are your strategic advantages that allow you to deliver on this value promise in ways competitors cannot easily match?

Think of these components as the design elements of your business model that ensure that customers trust your value promise. They also ensure that no competitor can easily copy nor deliver on your promise. Many companies forget Decision 4. They think that the promise is all that is needed—communicate the promise in new marketing materials—and forget the implications for how the company must work and what it must accomplish. The actual value proposition in the customers' minds is still the old one. When they hear the new one, it is first with interest but then with anger as they feel it is spin, not reality. There can be no new value proposition without new evidence to support it.

Famous Footwear defined its value proposition to women buying shoes for the family around success with the shoe shopping experience and with the emotions that accompany a woman's meeting family needs and her own needs. It created changes that demonstrated that Famous Footwear would deliver on its promise, such as implementing a new store layout and look, focusing store personnel on customer satisfaction, and adding a new service—shipping shoes free of charge to the customer from Famous Footwear's warehouse if the needed size was not on the shelf. These changes reinforced existing elements of Famous Footwear's business such as easy in-and-out parking due to the stores' locations.

In a similar way, there can be no emotion to a brand if there are no tangible legs supporting the brand. A classic example of this is Johnson & Johnson. It took Tylenol off the retailers' shelves and created new safety mechanisms on bottled medicine following a product-tampering scare in 1982 in order to reinforce the "safe" emotion its brand communicates.

Making the Four Decisions

There is no easy formula for deciding on the strategically differentiated business model that, once executed, will propel your company out of commodity competition and keep it there. The path to a strategically differentiated business model is seldom linear. In fact, because key decisions are often interdependent, you may find yourself feeling as if you are circling a decision more than approaching it straight on. Be patient. Strategic thinking often begins with conceptual thinking that is a different process than the analytical mind-set managers use to break a problem or project down into its component parts.

The hard part is having your team look at opportunities and select combinations of answers to the four strategy decisions that collectively define a new business model you can adopt to secure faster growth and higher profits. What makes this work hard is that the four business model decisions are interdependent—you cannot make them in isolation. This interconnection is important because *the relationship between where you compete and why you win is at the very heart of creating a strategically differentiated business model.*

For example, the *target market* you select must appreciate your *differentiated value promise*, the basis of your differentiation. There are times when you cannot deliver on your *differentiated value promise* without changing the *business you are in.* In commodity markets, you must either broaden your offering or significantly narrow it to deliver superior value. Sometimes, to deliver superior value, you need to significantly narrow your target market to be able to offer something that is truly superior. Finally, a differentiated value promise is a pipe dream without advantages and attributes that create the higher value.

Your task, therefore, is to select the combination of the four strategic decisions that define your business model. To be maximally effective in pulling or keeping you out of commodity markets, your strategically differentiated business model must create a unique market space—building a new industry or product category, a new value chain, or a new value proposition that no other company has yet captured.

Prioritizing Risks and Opportunities: Drawing Implications from the Strategic Assessment

The greatest value of the strategic assessment comes from prioritizing the risks and opportunities that the process revealed. Designing a strategically differentiated business model, whether an evolution from the current one or a significant redefinition, requires making decisions about where to compete and how to win that minimize risks and maximize synergistic opportunities.

BROADEN YOUR TEAM AGAIN

Just as we advised using a broader team during the strategic assessment, we recommend broadening it *again,* and even wider than before. Include your regular leadership team, the people included in the strategic assessment work, plus any others you think can offer new perspectives on this work. Why go broader still? Because enlarging the group will deepen the overall understanding of the risks and opportunities facing your company and your potential strategic positioning opportunities.

Narrow down the list of risks and opportunities.

Return to the list of risks and opportunities established in Step 3's strategic assessment. The next task is to narrow down this list to make it more manageable. There are various ways to do this.

- *Assign "quick hits" to operational managers.* You will have likely uncovered some no-brainer near-term (this year) tactical risks and opportunities that should be assigned to the ongoing operations and sales and marketing teams to address. Remove these from the list after assigning them to the appropriate people.

- *Group together risks that convey the same concept or are symptoms of the same deep cause.* For example, if a competitor can offer a "best-price guarantee" and engage in low-ball pricing to beat you because of their lower-cost structure, group these two risks into one risk—"competitor leverages lower-cost structure advantage via price guarantees and low-ball pricing."

- *Group together combinations of like opportunities.* As an example, you might have identified a number of new product opportunities that can be grouped into a "broaden the product line" strategy with subpoints for each opportunity.

- *Group together synergistic/complementary combinations.* As an example, you might have identified a number of new service opportunities you can offer alongside your product. These can be grouped into a "redefine the product offering to embrace complementary services" opportunity with subpoints for each service.

- *Rule out opportunities that are absolutely outside the scope of what you want to do with your company.* However, don't rule out an opportunity simply because "we don't know how." Just because you don't know *how* now doesn't mean you can't learn or find a partner to provide the needed addition to your scope. The more opportunities you rule out, the fewer growth and differentiation options you'll have. Great strategies stretch companies. The detailed how-to may not be available at the start. Be open. For example, an architectural firm may not want to become a construction firm, but they must be open to the opportunity of partnering with one on a regular basis if client needs demand more collaboration between builders and designers.

Prioritize the list.

Having narrowed your list of risks and opportunities, you must then prioritize them in terms of the potential magnitude of impact on your company's financial and marketplace performance as well as whether this impact will occur in the near term or long term.

Start by categorizing each risk and opportunity and sorting them according to what strategic decision they impact (see Table 4.1).

	WHERE YOU COMPETE		WHY YOU WIN	
	Target market and situation	What business you are in	Differentiated value promise	Attributes and advantages
Risks				
Opportunities				

TABLE 4.1 *Categorizing potential risks and opportunities*

Once you've sorted them this way, you can prioritize the risks and opportunities in terms of the potential magnitude of impact on your company's financial and marketplace performance. Also identify whether a risk is near-term or long-term. The most dangerous risks are both near-term and high impact, as you have the least opportunity to reduce them and they will have the greatest effect. However, be sure to look at every situation carefully. Remember, it is not uncommon for a risk to also be an opportunity!

- *Risk prioritization.* Analyze risks according to these characteristics:
  - *Probability* they will occur
  - *Magnitude* of impact if they occur

- *Opportunity prioritization.* You should prioritize opportunities (high, medium, and low) according to the following:
  - *Attractiveness* (What is the relative magnitude of financial return and relative time frame for payback?)
  - *Feasibility* (Can we do it?)
  - *Defensibility* (If we did it, could we defend our position?)
  - *Near versus long term* (The most attractive opportunities are near-term and high return.)

By effectively identifying, evaluating, and prioritizing your risks and opportunities and categorizing them according to the four business model decisions, you will get the highest return from your strategic assessment process.

The Next Level: Exploring the Strategic Decisions

There are a number of strategies you can use for exploring the options.

STRATEGIES FOR DECISION 1: *Choose your target market.*

- Choose the target market(s) that benefits from your existing or potential core competencies.
- Choose a distinct target market that is currently under- or overserved.
- Choose a target market that is not yet buying your categories or products because they're overdesigned for their needs.

- Grow sales and market share by targeting new situations—don't leave situations open for new entrants to capture.

STRATEGIES FOR DECISION 2: Choose what business to be in.

- Broaden your definition of your niche.
- Narrow your definition of your niche.

STRATEGIES FOR DECISION 3: Define a differentiated value promise.

- Eliminate customers' compromises and frustrations.
- Focus on customer benefits, not the attributes of your offering or the advantages of your business.
- Avoid meaningless differentiation!

STRATEGIES FOR DECISION 4: Define and develop strategic advantages.

- Build core competencies that allow you to deliver on your value promise in ways competitors cannot easily copy.
- Reinvent the value chain.

You can use any combination of strategies that fit your situation—you're not limited to one strategy per decision. Remember, as you go, to keep track of your ideas. At this point, the goal is *not* to actually make these decisions. Rather, you want to shed light upon those factors or issues that should feed into the business model decisions you make.

The rest of this step describes these various options and how you can use them to explore the implications of different business models. As you work through these questions, be sure to record any ideas that come to mind. We like using a format as in Table 4.2. For each insight, push the idea all the way into a business model.

For example, if you have an insight into a new target market, be sure to also think about the offering you would bring to this target market, the situations where you would be best able to compete, the value proposition, and the evidence you would have. Doing this work with each idea will help you unearth the strongest new business model.

TABLE 4.2 *Tracking business model idea*

BUSINESS MODEL COMPONENT		BUSINESS MODEL Idea #1	BUSINESS MODEL Idea #2
Who is our target market?	Target market description		
	Situations		
What business are we in—offering scope?	Scope of offering		
	Revenue exchange		
What is our value proposition?			
What will be our key evidence that we can deliver on our value proposition (even if we have to still build these skills)?			
What key risks will this model address?			
What key opportunities will this model address?			

Strategic Decision 1: Choose Your Target Market

Your company's target market defines what customer groups are strategic in terms of how you will design your offering and operate to meet their needs. Remember in Step 3 when you grouped customers into segments based on needs that vary from one group to another? To choose your target market, decide to which groups you can deliver the greatest differentiated benefits and highest value. Niche companies can be very successful financially because they have focused on a narrow target market. They are better positioned to meet the target's needs than companies trying to satisfy multiple target markets. If scale advantages are important, then multiple market segments are often advised.

Many leadership teams, especially those in companies with high capital costs or significant revenue growth requirements, are usually concerned about losing any business whatsoever. They view the concept of target markets as being restrictive, interpreting the principle as forcing them to turn down lucrative business. If your company is in that position, it's important to realize that we're not advocating that you strategize yourself into bankruptcy. Rather, if you're truly dedicated to getting out of commodity competition, you have to determine your most strategic target market (the segment of customers for whom you are willing to make business investments to better meet their needs). This investment may include increasing assets, redesigning your offering or how you operate your business, and developing organizational skills. But even after you choose a target market, you can always seek and accept capacity-filling business from customers outside your target market as long as you are not redesigning your business to meet their needs.

Here are four strategies for selecting a target market:

STRATEGY 1.1: *Choose the target markets that most benefit from your existing or potential core competencies.*

In order to thrive, your organization needs to offer customers benefits they value and that are not easily copied by your competition. Therefore, you should reach out to the target market you can best benefit. Remember that your profitability depends not just on market size and awareness of your company but also on the percentage of the market that will consider you and choose you over the competition. Strong core competencies create high consideration and win rates. Finfrock D-M-C's decision to sell to owners stemmed from its understanding that benefits such as life cycle cost, reduced risk, and speed to market mattered the most to building owners, not the company's original target market of general contractors.

STRATEGY 1.2: *Choose a distinct target market that is currently under- or overserved.*

Distinct means you can clearly separate the needs of this market from the needs of other related markets. *Underserved* means no one is meeting those needs; *overserved* means what is available is overbuilt and overpriced relative to the market's genuine needs.

Growing your revenues and profits requires taking market share from another competitor or creating an entirely new category of offering that has no current competition. How do you do this? One way is to identify a subset of an existing market that is really not like the rest of the market. The discount retailer Target decided that not all discount store shoppers are alike. Some strongly preferred a design-driven look for their home or wardrobe. Differentiating their offering by adding a design flair while maintaining competitive prices created an upscale look that lured customers away from Wal-Mart.

STRATEGY 1.3: *Choose a target market that is not yet buying your categories or products because they're overdesigned for their needs.*

Sometimes the best target market is a group that is not yet in your market but could be, if you were willing to design an offering to meet their needs. There are few customers early in the life cycle of new technologies or product concepts. A reliable, easy-to-use option, like Apple's IPod, creates new customers. Customers also stay out due to cost. Pottery Barn is a more affordable solution than hiring in-home interior designer services.

STRATEGY 1.4: *Grow sales and market share by targeting new situations—don't leave situations open for new entrants to capture.*

It is a myth to think that a target market always has the same needs. It is much more realistic to think about different situations the target market may be in and recognize that each situation brings a completely different set of buying considerations.

Companies typically secure a market position by being the best choice for a specific target market situation. You can gain share of mind and share of pocketbook by expanding the range of situations you serve. Segmenting the market by situation can bring additional insights into the selection of target markets.

For example, a woman purchasing a frozen meal for herself will have different criteria than if she is purchasing a quick solution for her "meat and potatoes" husband she is leaving at home while she goes off on a business trip. Stouffer's Lean Cuisine does a great job with the former, while Hungry Man frozen entrees and Hormel refrigerated entrees are better for the latter.

At the same time, it is vital that you defend your position with the target market against competitors. One of the hallmarks of Oscar Mayer's Lunchables success (a business as large as many companies) is that it quickly moved from packaged lunches to snacks, so as to preclude a new competitor's taking its concept to another meal occasion. It is now extending this concept into a "lunchables" for adults, a collection of food items and a microwavable tray to create a fresh, hot deli sandwich.

Strategic Decision 2: Choose What Business to Be In

Under what heading do you want your target market to place your company's brochures? How do you want your customers to describe your business to others?

What business you are in defines the products, services, technologies, and geographies that are inside and outside your scope of offerings. If you do not define the business you are in strategically, you lose opportunities to step out from the pack of competitors who are selling essentially the same product or solution. In commodity markets, redefining the business you are in is often the ticket for moving into real strategic differentiation.

Imagine your customers seeing your company as the *only* company in a certain category. Now, imagine that that category is highly valuable to them and other companies like them. You would be in what amounts to a monopoly position. Your company would be in a file and folder all to yourself.

All too often, companies take their definition of products and services as a given: "We are printers, always have been printers, and always will be printers." Or, "We are a women's clothing line." This myopic and rigid view leads to lost opportunity. For example, defining a new frame of reference for a printing company, such as "We are your main resource, supply room, and mailing center for up-to-date company brochures and other product literature," gives your business a new, unique perspective in the eyes of your customers. "We are image enhancers" opens a whole new way to think about women's clothing and the categories a women's clothing line might offer.

Sometimes, a company has difficulty finding a unique business definition. In this case, all its differentiation will have to come from having a value proposition that is stronger than that of competitors with the same business definition. This can often be a less defensible position (vis-à-vis competitors copying you) than creating a vastly different scope of products and services.

The most common ways to better define what business you want to be in are to either broaden your current definition of your current niche or narrow it.

STRATEGY 2.1: *Broaden your definition of your niche.*

Redefine your product or service niche by identifying the larger business of which it is a part. In doing so, you expand your scope to offer solutions to the higher-level problems your target customers face. When your business is narrowly defined and selling to the right target market, but remains stuck in a commodity market rut, it is next to impossible to break out of commodity competition without a broadening of your offering. Why? The broader the offering, the greater the opportunity to deliver value. Imagine going to a different market for each individual product on your grocery-shopping list. The success of the supermarket concept, indeed many retailers' concepts, relied on the value of a broad offering.

STRATEGY 2.2: *Narrow your definition of your niche.*

If your business is already broadly defined, identify the product or service niche within your overall business that is working the best and build on it. It is easy to overestimate just how valuable one-stop shopping is, especially when purchasing agents in your customers' businesses or at the retail chains are doing everything possible to have you sell category by category. When breadth brings complexity to your business without providing any real advantage to customers, it is time to narrow your offering. One of Sears's core issues was that it tried to sell products that did not belong together (clothes and hardware) in the same department store setting. Businesses also end up with too broad an offering when they grow in ways that lead the business to be in multiple market segments, each with distinctly different needs.

TOO BROAD OR TOO NARROW?

Rather than jump to a conclusion, it's better to explore both of these options and what they would mean for your company.

Strategic Decision 3: Define a Differentiated Value Promise

Your company's *differentiated value promise* summarizes the superior benefits (that do not compromise your margins) that will lead customers to select your company. It is vital that the value promise be defined in terms that matter to customers.

Consider these three strategies for determining your differentiated value promise.

STRATEGY 3.1: *Eliminate customers' compromises and frustrations.*

When answering Question 6 in Step 3 (on page 80), you should have unearthed the compromises and frustrations customers encounter when buying or using your industry's products and services and what jobs they wish someone would do for them. Most times, customers assume there is no way to reduce those compromises and frustrations or to outsource tasks on their long to-do list. Therefore, they don't communicate what they would like to change. *Gaps between what is currently available and what may actually be possible create openings for differentiating your company and its offerings.*

Whole Foods is a great example of a company that entered an industry where it is hard to make a buck and has succeeded in obtaining runaway growth and profitability. It has made it easy for the food buyer to find fresh, organic, and local produce without having to spend a large amount of time shopping. Another compromise solving strategy comes from traditional grocers. Computer ordering and home delivery of groceries save working parents needed time and often provide healthier meals than restaurant takeout.

STRATEGY 3.2: *Focus on customer benefits, not the attributes of your offering or the advantages of your business.*

Let's draw distinctions between three terms that are commonly interchanged when they should not be.

- **Benefits** are items of value to *customers*. Benefits are why customers get excited about a product or service. They are defined in the customers' terms. They are how the customer is better off in tangible and emotional terms.

- **Attributes**, or features, and **advantages** are about *your company*. They are aspects of your offering or company that ensure that you can deliver benefits.

ATTRIBUTES ALONE DON'T
CREATE SUSTAINED VICTORIES

Attributes are how you translate your advantages into your offering. Your marketing and sales staff, and certainly customers when they evaluate whether or not you can deliver on your promised benefits, will care greatly about how you define the attributes of your offerings—but their value is wholly dependent on the advantages you build into your company that competitors cannot easily copy.

Customers will not care about your attributes or advantages until they know they are interested in their derived benefits. Companies forget this all the time. They build promotions, sales events, and advertising around attributes and advantages—as if customers really care. They do not, at least until they're excited about your benefit. Do you really want to know how a plane works, or is knowing there is a 99 percent on-time record with the best safety statistics in the industry more important to you?

Companies too often focus only on their product attributes and internal advantages. Instead, they should think of delivering customer benefits and indirect cost savings for the customer. When companies analyze why they win business only from an internal view, they work under the illusion of being better than their competition without customers agreeing. For example, lots of companies try to differentiate on quality, failing to recognize that quality has become the norm for being considered, not a benefit suggesting superior value. They are promising customers something they already have enough of, and their reaction is, "Sorry, I'm very content with my current brand and I don't want to spend the time learning about yours."

Instead, you must offer benefits defined from the customers' perspective—something they cannot get enough of and, ideally, something other companies are not yet promising. At this point of maturity in the car industry, warranties and a basic level of quality in new cars are sufficiently pervasive that the promise of less risk does not shift consumer loyalty. We are, however, likely to be attracted to time savings through effortless service and fuel savings, as brands such as Lexus and Toyota's Prius, respectively, have shown. If customers could buy your offerings and be guaranteed benefits while never knowing anything about your industry or company, they likely would chose to know nothing about your industry or company. Remember, business customers are interested in their own offerings and their own customers. Consumers are interested in their own and loved ones' well-being, including feeling altruistic when buying from companies that are good corporate citizens. (The growing interest in buying from socially responsible companies is a subject discussed later in the book.) *Their only interest in your attributes and advantages is as the proof that you can provide them your promised benefits.*

STRATEGY 3.3: *Avoid meaningless differentiation.*

The endgame is profits, not revenue. The benefits you offer must be worth more to your customer than it will cost you to provide them. Otherwise, you run the risk of creating differentiation without profitability. At the same time, do not rule out meaningful potential benefits because you are unsure if you can deliver

---

THE IMPORTANCE OF MARKET RESEARCH

Your need for truly differentiated benefits underscores the importance of market research. Finding out what frustrates or hinders customers' success or takes more of the customers' time than it is worth to them is the most important market research objective your company can have. Getting the answer is not always easy, as compromises and frustrations and basic assumptions about what companies do and do not do have become so ingrained in customers that they may fail to even recognize or acknowledge them. If you didn't already do so when completing Step 3, open the door to deeper learning by having your business customers define how they create success for *their* customers. For consumers, ask what creates well-being in their lives. Then, as they discuss each stage of their process, ask how your industry as a whole inhibits or contributes to their success or well-being.

them in a cost-effective manner. Experimentation beats delays when it comes to differentiation.

A classic example of meaningless differentiation is when companies move to a quality or feature level or breadth of line that exceeds what customers really want. This is occurring in many retail segments where customers are finally screaming for simplification, clear-cut choices, and ease-of-use products when facing a plethora of line extensions for a product category or brand. Does each of the variants of toothbrushes really make a difference? Do we really need more multigrain bread options on the grocer's shelf when food shoppers aren't really sure what food to buy for tonight's dinner and next week's lunches? The complexity in offering many product variations often costs the company more in manufacturing and supply-chain costs than it gains in market share. While a brand preference may help consumers save time, too many choices within a brand can create the same level of frustration as can too many brand options.

Meaningless differentiation often turns out to be nothing more than confusing, frustrating, and alienating to customers. That is why it is vital that companies focus on delivering genuine benefits and measurable value to their target markets.

Strategic Decision 4: Define and Develop Strategic Advantages

Advantages are unique organizational design elements of your company that ensure that it will deliver on its value promise. They are the key differentiation points between your organization's skills and how it operates and those of the competition. They ensure that your value promise is really a value *guarantee* that competitors cannot readily copy. Indeed, companies that are secure in their advantages win even more business by making formal guarantees that their competitors cannot match without adverse consequences to their profitability.

The two components of how you win—value promise plus advantages—are interdependent. To deliver on your value promise, you must have the advantages that create a value your competitors cannot easily match.

Let's look at a couple of key strategies for creating winning advantages.

STRATEGY 4.1: *Build core competencies that ensure you will fulfill your value promise in ways competitors cannot easily copy.*

The core competencies you identified in Step 3 are perhaps the most important advantage you have over your competition. As discussed there, a core competency is a high-level skill of the entire organization. It is something that the organization (versus one person or one department) does well that

- Matters to customers because it creates benefits and therefore value.

- Cannot be easily copied by the competition (because the competency relies on learning, culture, and how your organization is designed).

- Establishes where you are superior to the competition.

- Allows your company to successfully move into new markets (geographic, target customer, product or service offering).

A core competency lets you create the benefits that customers want and leads them to choose you over the competition. Without a core competency in place or under development, your value promise is, at best, a wish, with a low probability that you will deliver. You'll end up with great ad copy and little else.

There are other advantages that help to create the core competency and provide additional benefits to your company. For example, the organization's culture can be a key advantage. If you promise the target market a steady stream of new offerings, you must have an innovative culture. To become a core competency, such an innovative culture must cut across multiple departments, not just be the sole domain of R&D, and be focused on customer value creation. (We will take up the subject of culture in Step 8.)

The reality is that most firms that find themselves in commodity market quicksand lack the complete collection of skills and cultural elements needed to have a core competency. As you evaluate your company's strategic advantages, pay attention to the skills you will need to develop in order to build a true core competency. Use the results of your strategic assessment to identify skills that can be effectively and efficiently developed into a core competency. Think about changes in how your people work with one another and external partners that could further advance these skills. Compared to a consortium of companies brought together for one or more building projects, Finfrock D-M-C could more closely align engineering, sales, precast manufacturing, and construction decisions through one integrated firm to better meet the building owner's needs while reducing the duration, risk, and cost of the building project. This core competency created Finfrock D-M-C's differential advantage and resulted in a company offering unique value to its target market.

STRATEGY 4.2: *Reinvent the value chain.*

The value chain represents all the process steps from material acquisition to the final product reaching the end-user, who may actually be your customers' customer or beyond. It includes both your own firm's activities and those of suppliers, customers, and partners. Where you are in the value chain is typically the result of past decisions.

Redefining the value chain—such as by pulling out steps that do not add value to customers—often reduces costs and increases benefits. Dell Computer built wealth by selling direct to the consumer and getting so good at the direct model that copycats were left in the dust for years. American Girl cut out the toy distribution channel, and its direct sales to girls and their parents allowed the company to better position the many benefits of the doll and book line. In fact, its story-filled catalog became part of the offering for the dolls' fans. Retail American Girl stores, historical site experiences, books, and clothing for dolls and doll owners alike, along with the dolls, built a unique, stellar brand.

Pulling It All Together: The Art of Designing a Strategically Differentiated Business Model

From the list of ideas you've generated so far, you want to further develop two to six alternative business models, each representing different sets of decisions about where to compete and how to win. You can then review and compare these options to make the final decision. To provide structure to this process, you may find it helpful to do the following:

- Use Table 4.2 on page 114 to record business model ideas that surfaced in Step 3 and to suggest still other options.
- Discuss each business model idea.

- Examine the potential risk(s) you associated with each option and decide which options best address your most significant risks.
- Examine the potential opportunity(ies) you associated with each option and decide which options best address your most significant opportunities.
- Look across the various models you are considering. Are there ways to blend the models so as to strengthen your ability to seize opportunities without reducing your ability to address risks?

- Allow time for thinking and evaluating.

- Make a preliminary selection of options.

- Explore ways to combine models again, being careful to ensure that they are synergistic. For example, serving two target markets may do a better job of seizing opportunities, but if the evidence you need for each and the value proposition you need for each are in conflict, you cannot easily combine these two models and expect to execute effectively.

- Rate each option against the *seven vital requirements* listed in the following paragraph.

The seven vital requirements collectively create an unbeatable strategically differentiated business model. How well will your proposed model(s) do the following?

1. *Reduce competitive intensity.* The new market position must make you considerably different and of higher value than you were, thereby enhancing your margins. You are no longer one of many very similar alternatives for your customers.

2. *Be defensible.* No other competitor is able to automatically beat you at your game. Market positions that create entire new industries or product categories are the very best examples of being defensible. (The key to defensibility rests in the next standard.)

3. *Have a defensible value proposition.* Rely on learning and knowledge, not just resources that can be acquired by your competitors; otherwise, the value proposition will be very hard to defend.

4. *Offer growth prospects.* Market positions that open up multiple avenues for future growth are far more attractive than those that offer few.

5. *Be feasible to execute.* The model must build from the organization's existing strengths and rely on acquisitions, partnerships, or internal developments that are obtainable even though the specific game plan for proceeding may not yet be clear.

6. *Retain a substantial percentage of your current customer base.* Enough current business must be retained to ensure that the organization does not enter a financial crisis from significant revenue declines.

7. *Be accurately aligned with external realities.* The new positioning must be aligned with emerging trends that will have a significant impact on your business. It must minimize the risks and take advantage of the opportunities previously identified.

Have faith. The best business model probably won't appear all at once in a blinding flash of inspiration. Keep digging. Give your team some time to let ideas simmer. After working through the business model options the first time, come back in a week or two and the choices will be clearer. Insights you did not immediately see from the strategic assessment may become more apparent. Some companies take one to three years to genuinely clarify their strategically differentiated business model to achieve the focus and clarity that creates a winning position.

Leading Your Team through Key Decision Making

The case study presented at the beginning of this chapter and others in this book should have given you a gut feeling for the magnitude of change that is likely when your goal is to define a business model that is strategically differentiated and sustainable. This is anything *but* business as usual.

As a consequence, you and your entire leadership team are going to be yanked forcibly from your comfort zones. Even with all its flaws and risks, your current business model—which your leadership team knows intimately—often feels a lot safer than constructing a new one that has not yet been tested. Every possible reason why the company cannot change will show up sometime during discussions related to this step. You can't avoid them. This work will force you and your team to face the genuine prospect of change.

Identify symptoms of resistance.

You *will* encounter resistance. And it will come from many sides. First, there will be the groups that argue that the only problem you need to solve is doing better with the current model. The more fear a leader feels, the more he or she will point fingers at someone else's domain—blaming manufacturing or marketing or sales or service or purchasing, claiming if *they* would just start doing what is needed, then this leader's own area would not need to change.

Another group will find all the reasons why the newly proposed business models will not work. These people can see all the flaws in a new model, yet they have no willingness to explore how to avoid them.

The CFO and possibly others may argue that you lack the money to make the investments to build a new business model.

And the strongest push back will come from leaders who say, "If we do that, our customers (suppliers, employees—anyone but competitors) will walk away from us, and then where will the company be?"

Some leaders may become real proponents during this step. Be cautious here as well—if their optimism is too great, the rest of the team will push back even more, convinced that the positive leaders have not a single clue about what a new business model might entail.

Overcome the resistance.

Avoid direct arguments that, in an absence of facts, are likely to polarize people even more. Instead, return to a discussion of what people really want to create in the company. What level of success do they want? What will make them wake up excited for every weekday morning? What do they want to leave as their legacy to the next generation of leaders?

Then ask if the current business model will take them to their aspirations. If leaders are honest, they will admit that the business model cannot, if the business is headed into commodity competition. Once you have unlocked this insight, you offer the new business model as a possible focusing point where the leadership team can work its way out of price-based competition's grip. Tell the leaders that by working together, you'll unearth the weaknesses in any new model and make midcourse corrections. But the team needs to start somewhere, and the new business model is the most promising place to start. Without a new business model, all you'll have are dreams of a stronger company, but no way of achieving them.

Conclusion

A new strategically differentiated business model moves you closer to true differentiation and moves your business *beyond price*. Yet more work is needed before implementation of the model commences. If the rest of the management team and associates neither understand nor agree to your business model, nothing will change in the direction you desire. Steps 5 and 6 outline the work in which the leadership team needs to engage to build enthusiasm about and commitment to the new strategically differentiated business model.

STEP 4 KEY POINTS

Turn your strategic assessment into a bold step toward profitability by designing a new strategically differentiated business model. New answers to where you compete and why you win will pull you out of commodity market quicksand.

Desired goals:

The leadership team decides on four key, interrelated strategic questions that collectively point to the market space you want to own. These decisions define your strategically differentiated business model:

✔ Who is/are our strategic target market(s), and in what target market situation(s) are we the best choice?

✔ What business are we in as defined by the customer (points toward our products and services)?

✔ What is/are our differentiated value promise(s) that our competitors cannot easily duplicate?

✔ What advantages and attributes will ensure that we can deliver on our value promise far better than any other competitor?

Keys to success:

✔ Be ruthlessly honest about what your business can and cannot do now, as well as what could be realistically possible. It is far better to know you have no core competency than to pretend you do.

✔ Recognize that selecting a strategic positioning often starts with conceptual rather than analytical thinking and is not a linear process.

✔ Evaluate many different possibilities and decide on those that best meet preestablished criteria, including addressing the most important risks and opportunities facing your organization.

✔ Have patience while developing options for the four interrelated business model decisions.

✔ Realize that how you compete is not carved forever in stone but can be changed by you.

✔ Do not lose track of key economic principles (Step 1). Check every idea against them.

✔ Turn off judging and focusing on how you will execute until you are ready to evaluate final options. Too many terrific ideas can be defeated when you worry too early about how to execute them.

✔ You cannot be all things to all people. Sometimes you have to give up business to get business.

✔ Resist easy answers. Search for new, creative breakthrough ways of thinking about frame of reference and value promise.

✔ Stop giving away a core competency free of charge. Find a definition of your business—what it offers—and a target market that will ensure that you are paid for your specialized knowledge and expertise.

✔ Remember to never leave your most important strategic questions—where you compete and why you win—to history or serendipity.

The same business model will give you the same old results . . . or worse.

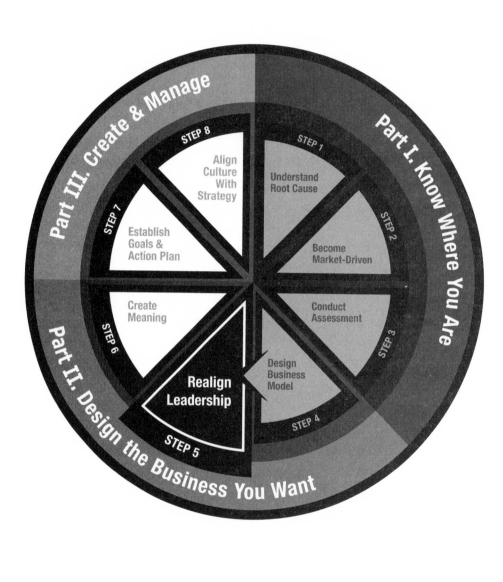

Step 5

Realign the Leadership Team

We can't solve problems by using the same kind of thinking we used when we created them. —Albert Einstein

As a new CEO, Ron was shocked at the culture he encountered when he took the reins of a window blind business. It seemed as if every decision that involved more than one department landed at his desk. This was quite a contrast from the company he had left. The internal focus of the company was also startling to Ron. Competition between departments was more intense than competition with the real competitors, other window blind and curtain companies.

Ron's first step was to bring the management team together to learn more about the marketplace and the company's position in the market. Together they forged a new business model—whose value proposition was to offer retail chain customers the best experience possible. This value proposition made a lot of sense given the high levels of dissatisfaction retailers had about selling a complicated product and consumers had about making a product selection. The company would need to dramatically improve quality and supply chain performance, make the offering easier for retail salespeople to sell, and offer new looks to meet customers' desires to refresh their homes or offices. The business model also required the company to serve more channels, so that however the consumer wanted to buy (in a store or with an in-home designer, for example), he or she could find one of the company's brands.

With a new value proposition that managers were excited about, Ron then charged his leadership team with its execution. One thing was clear, it would never create the changes the company needed to make if the culture of the company did not change, starting with how leaders made decisions. The next step was to write a charter for the role of the leadership team in executing the strategy. In essence, Ron was rewriting the job descriptions of his senior leaders, both individually and when they worked as a team.

In addition to the charter, Ron established a series of monthly review meetings in which managers of different product categories and key processes of the business reported to the leadership team against plans. In the meetings of the senior team, Ron and his team talked through issues that cut across the different parts of the company. In these discussions, Ron modeled what collaborative decision making looked like. Over time, senior leaders were able to address many cross-departmental issues on their own, freeing some of Ron's time to tackle projects only he could best lead.

Like Ron's company, your company *can* escape from a commodity market and regain control of your pricing and your future. But to do this, you need more than a new business model. You must recognize behaviors, practices, and attitudes within your leadership team that could stand in the way and then take positive action to refocus and reenergize the team.

Waiting for the market to change is not going to allow the organization to break out of or steer clear of commodity competition. Senior management must take responsibility for results rather than falling back on the excuses of a tough industry or poor economic climate. The leadership team must do the one thing no one else in the company can do—figure out how to break free of commodity competition. This work must be the leadership team's first and most important responsibility—not the cost-cutting, scheduling, and quality improving operational management that previously absorbed the leadership team's agenda. No other team represents the whole of the organization, so no other team can fundamentally transform how the company competes in its markets.

If the leadership team does not strategically differentiate the business (or the alternative—build advantages that ensure that it becomes the lowest cost supplier in a market), it will have failed in that most important role.

This chapter presents a five-part plan to make sure that your leadership team can step up to the plate and make the new business model a reality.

1. Recognize factors and behaviors that may keep your business stuck in commodity markets.

2. Reemphasize where leadership adds value to the organization that no other team can add.

3. Embrace conflict *and* collaboration.

4. Focus the CEO on increasing the leadership capacity of the senior leadership team and its members versus making the team's decisions.

5. Develop new norms for the leadership team's behavior, documented in a new leadership team charter.

YOU ARE HERE

Links to previous steps: Based on your analysis of the strategic assessment, you should have clear decisions about your company's business model. This creates the motivation that leaders need in order to change their behavior and strengthen strategic leadership skills.

Expected outcome: The leadership team will be fully committed with the new strategically differentiated direction, understand what forces may work against the shift, and therefore know what needs to be done to bring about the change.

Who is involved: This step is the exclusive work of the leadership team.

Why this step is important: Changing corporate direction requires strong, united leadership. Otherwise, you run the danger that splinters will form within the company that will distract you from the essential work of the company and create misalignments among parts of the business. Getting your leadership team aligned sets the stage for rapid progress.

Recognize Factors and Behaviors That May Keep You Stuck in Commodity Markets

Many leaders in or approaching commodity markets slide into survival management thinking that drives their company further into competing on price. In survival management, the leadership team and its members overemphasize cost-cutting operational management at the opportunity cost of creating strategic differentiation.

Does this sound familiar? Perhaps you recognize some of these symptoms:

- The vast majority of the leadership team's conversation focuses on resolving operational issues to keep the work flowing or on near-term planning (at most, one year).

- Potential actions for improving low profit margins, or issues related to these actions, continue to reappear on the agenda.

- Depending on the openness of the culture, key issues that interfere with the success of the company, or are undermining trust among leaders, may or may not reach leadership team meetings where they can be addressed by the whole of the team.

- Over time, relationships between different leadership team members have suffered as blame gets shifted from one leader to another for recurring operational, profit, and revenue issues.

- There is too much competition among the leadership team members. Not enough time is spent on discussing and strategizing against the true competition.

- The less open and trusting the culture, the more undiscussables[11] there are—issues people talk about around the water cooler or over a meal, but never in front of the people who are either creating or could solve the issue.

- A growing lack of trust in the leadership team makes it harder to talk about the strategic issues the company faces. If they are talked about at all, the discussion is guarded and superficial (e.g., "It's not my department's fault," and "What can we do? It's the market we're in.").

- The CEO feels like everyone is working harder and harder just to stay even. And this is true.

- The group takes the rules of the marketplace as given and never talks about how to change these rules.

- The entire team focuses its primary effort on achieving near term revenue targets and making process improvements to retain or regain profitability. No one feels there is any time available in the day or month to step back and rethink how they might get out of the rut in which they find themselves and their business.

- With leadership focused on short-term goals, individuals are becoming frustrated, and the company as a whole is not advancing.

- You feel tired mentally, physically, and emotionally.

The team may take great pride in its heroics and how much it is getting done in terms of resolving day-to-day operational issues and meeting demanding operational needs. But once stuck in survival thinking, the team feels like it is in a daily 24-7-365 battle. The CEO, leadership team, and their direct reports are undoubtedly growing weary.

If these things are happening at your company, the sad truth is that your competitors ultimately may be dictating your organization's future direction. When this happens, you can be sure that your competitors' aspirations for your company are unlikely to be in your best interests.

There is nothing wrong with cost-cutting operational management. It is a necessary condition for success. But when it becomes the full-time activity of the leadership team, leaders are not doing the work they alone can do—creating a strategically differentiated business.

There are four key factors that keep leadership teams stuck in survival mode.

1. *Mistaken beliefs.* The leadership team assumes that the way the market works now is the way the market will always work. Such rigid beliefs about how the market works are the greatest impediment to genuine change. By taking the rules of the market as a given, there is no urgency for the leadership team to redesign the way the company competes and

operates. "Success" is seen as improving operational performance in order to offer the lowest price or to catch temporary profit improvements or to make tactical moves that gain market share temporarily.

2. *Lack of skills.* The leadership team knows it should focus on changing and improving the company, but members do not know how to truly escape or avoid commodity markets. Rather than try and risk failing, they remain busy with overflowing in-baskets, arguing that there is no time to do anything differently.[12] The underlying thinking becomes: "It is better to succeed at what we know than fail at something new."

3. *Lack of willpower.* Some leaders know how to innovate a business model, but they fear the organizational and personal implications. Others are looking for a quick fix but, absent that, will not set change in motion.

4. *Fear of short-term losses.* Day-to-day business pressures feel so great that leaders fear initiating fundamental change that might result in unacceptable short-term losses. Such fear keeps leaders stuck in survival mode.

When leaders stay stuck primarily or exclusively in operational management without strategically differentiating the company, they limit the company's potential. Morale and initiative fall as the organization underperforms relative to its inherent potential. Good people—the kind you need to break out of and stay out of commodity competition—start to leave, or even refuse to come to your company in the first place. Cleaning up this mess requires nothing short of an entirely new view of the role of the leadership team in creating business success.

Reemphasize Where Leadership Adds Value to the Organization That No Other Team Can Add

The best way out of these traps is to refocus your team on the most critical role of leadership: defining and guiding the organization toward its desired future. All operational management is then in pursuit of this direction, not just this quarter's or year's budget. Start by getting a solid grip on what leadership team responsibilities will most benefit the whole organization. Typically, these include both strategic and operational categories, but they all fall under the fundamental "guidance role" the leadership team serves.

The critical responsibilities include the following:

- Establish the organization's
  - Purpose (why it exists, including but not limited to making money).
  - Vision (what outcome it wants to reach five to eight years out).
  - Guiding principles or core values for how people conduct their work. (*These elements will be discussed in Step 6.*)

- Establish where and how the company wants to win business. This is the most important strategic decision of the company and includes questions such as, "What business are we in?" and "Why will we be chosen by our target market(s) over other alternatives?" (*This was covered in Step 4.*)

- Ensure that the different parts of the organization are designed and aligned to win business the way the company wants to win business. (*This will be covered in Step 7.*) This includes the following:
  - Organizational structure
  - Core competency(ies) of the organization
  - Decisions on where the organization adds value rather than relying on partners and suppliers
  - Resource deployment
  - Priorities for process improvements and redesign
  - Annual goals
  - Measures and rewards

- Stay abreast of market changes and provide an atmosphere conducive to individual and organizational learning.

- Monitor organizational performance along multiple disciplines—financial, marketplace, operational, workplace environment, innovation, personnel, and so on.

- Create, review, and approve company policies.

- Model the desired corporate culture.

- Ensure that the organization is developing the skills and leaders needed to remain successful in the long term.

It may be that your leadership team is already doing all or most of these things. If so, congratulate yourself on having a properly focused team. If not, then you have some work to do to get your team refocused.

At this point, the goal is to simply get the team to agree that these *are* the most important responsibilities. This alignment is critical before you proceed with the work of implementing your new business model. The work will include both one-time changes needed to ensure that you have the capability and capacity to move in a new direction—such as redefining your purpose (see Step 6)—and making structural changes and adopting new practices needed to make sure you keep on top of the market. (Step 7 discusses these changes in detail.)

Embrace Conflict and Collaboration

When a leadership team steps into its inherent and vital guidance role, conflicts become a signal of alignment issues. When the leadership team is focused exclusively on operational management, conflicts are seen as a disruption to work flow, so efforts are often made to keep conflicts under the surface. In their guidance role, however, leaders welcome conflicts because they help the leadership team excel in identifying misalignments in the organization.

To create a thriving leadership team, you must understand the gift of conflict and the art of collaboration. Conflict—current or potential—is a signal of an alignment issue among interdependent parts. One part of the organization feels its ability to be successful in its role is, or will be, undermined by another part of the organization. The conflict might be a false alarm, based on misinterpretations or miscommunications. Or the conflict can be real, with definite unresolved differences between parts of the organization and their leaders.

Unresolved conflicts are like weeds in an organization. They grow and spread, becoming increasingly difficult to eradicate. Parts of the organization work at cross-purposes, reducing your potential value to customers and your differentiation. Conflict brought into the open and resolved through candid, strategic conversations reveals strategies to increase customer value.

When conflicts emerge in a new or small organization, they are typically much easier to handle. Everyone is familiar with the strategy, shares the vision, and is thinking along the same lines. The organization is flexible, as boundaries between the parts are fluid. People pull together to find solutions that work for the whole company.

As the organization grows, however, responsibilities are divided to promote both efficiency and effectiveness. Cultural norms start to develop that determine how conflicts get resolved. When leaders are in true agreement, you cannot observe the culture. Cultural norms exert their strongest hold when conflicts emerge.

There is a lot to learn by observing how conflicts are resolved or not resolved in your organization. By grasping this understanding, you can begin to build the collaboration skills and culture that will ultimately move you into a consistently successful organization because all the parts of the organization are aligned around its aim and desired strategic differentiation.

IDENTIFY OPERATIONAL VERSUS GUIDANCE MANAGEMENT

Most leaders agree that the responsibilities listed above fall into their laps. Unfortunately, all too often they mistake operational management as guidance work. Operational management keeps day-to-day work flowing; that is the responsibility of people who report to the leadership team. *Guidance work changes the design of the organization to ensure its long-term survival and prosperity.*

Fulfilling the guidance role keeps the company in a success-focused mentality and generates desired results. Stepping into the guidance role, therefore, is the first step in leaders breaking out of the survival thinking that commodity competition or rapidly approaching commoditization creates. When you do this, your focus shifts from looking mostly at financial performance to becoming vigilant about the company's value to its customers relative to the competition. The conversation shifts from "Will we make our numbers this quarter?" to "How do we genuinely differentiate ourselves from the competition?" and "How do we ensure that profits remain strong three years out?"

What are the styles of conflict resolution?

Leadership teams resolve their conflicts in one of six basic styles. The style that predominates defines one critical aspect of their culture. Usually, because other managers follow by example, the leadership team defines the culture of the organization as a whole. The only exception to this rule is when there are new leaders and an entrenched culture keeps teams from following the leaders' model. This exception is one of the reasons acquisitions and mergers fail when cultural fit is lacking.

1. *Competitive.* This is win/lose, with basic trust issues among leaders.

2. *Independent.* Each leader acts in his or her own group's best interests without consideration for other parts of the organization. This is silo culture at its worst. Since each group is self-reliant, groups tend to not think about trust as a corporate issue. Trust is irrelevant in this culture.

3. *Hierarchical.* The CEO calls the shots and resolves any conflict. The degree of trust and the willingness of leaders to be open depend on the CEO's style and the openness of the culture that he or she tries to form.

4. *Coordinating.* Leaders still act in their own best interests but alert others in order to keep the work flowing. A coordinating group acts like an independent group, but with more information sharing. Trust building is at its very basic stage as people try to coordinate their work and keep conflicts out of the CEO's responsibility to resolve.

5. *Cooperative.* Individual executives or departments absorb or share advantages and disadvantages of decisions so as to move the work along and preserve a sense of harmony. There is an "I'll scratch your back if you'll scratch mine" mentality. Trust is more clearly starting to develop. Conflicts are brought up, but in a way that does not challenge the mantle of politeness. Boundaries are clearly defined but have some give-and-take.

6. *Collaborative.* Leaders and their departments work side by side to resolve conflicts and manage interdependencies. They accept shared responsibility and accountability for outcomes of the company, not just their department. They make the best decisions to realize these outcomes, while also preserving and enhancing their working relationship. They act

COMPETITIVE CULTURE

INDEPENDENT CULTURE

HIERARCHICAL CULTURE

COORDINATING CULTURE

COOPERATIVE CULTURE

COLLABORATIVE CULTURE

in ways that build more trusting and effective relationships. In a collaborative culture, boundaries are loose and executives are willing to change how they do things to move a shared effort forward. Conflicts, however charged, are brought to the surface and discussed openly to ensure trust continues to grow. The degree of openness is the best barometer of whether a leadership team works collaboratively or cooperatively.

Why is collaborative conflict resolution so important?

Collaborative conflict resolution is at the heart of a thriving leadership team and organization. There are two reasons for this.

1. *Better solutions.* In a culture of collaboration, teams try to eliminate the burden of one part of the organization's actions on other parts by working to find the solution that is best for all. The collaborative spirit also creates an environment of innovation where breakthrough thinking can even eliminate certain conflicts altogether—thus increasing the organization's capacity to accomplish its overall goals.

   Such breakthroughs are exactly what winning strategies are all about. They shatter historic compromises and trade-offs in the market. Rather than trade price for quality, speed for price, or a solution to a customer's task for spending large sums of money, organizations in which leadership works collaboratively create what customers value—such as enhanced quality, faster delivery, or a desired solution at lower prices.

2. *Faster execution of the new business model.* Leaders who work collaboratively and share ownership of alignment have the potential to excel in the guidance role. By accepting responsibility for alignment and committing to work through conflicts collaboratively, the leaders run their part of the organization on behalf of the team. In this capacity, the leader's role is to ensure that her part of the organization is working successfully with other parts of the organization to maximize overall success. Aligned organizations achieve higher resource efficiency and effectiveness.

Where change starts

Redefining a leader's role is the most powerful step a company can make to change focus from day-to-day operations into a strategic perspective. It is also a big step forward in creating a strategically differentiated business.

That all makes good sense, but how does it work out here in the real world?

To put all the pieces together, the CEO must initiate a conversation inside the leadership team about its role in the ultimate success of the organization. This dialogue will start to unlock the team from old behaviors. The leaders can then begin to craft a leadership team charter based on the key question: "What is our unique role in this organization—what work needs to be done that only our team can lead and accomplish?"

Together, they must first decide to tackle establishing the company's vision. The new driving purpose and visionary goal the leadership team established can be quite simple: In the case of Finfrock D-M-C, the initial vision of the company was, "Our company will realize the full potential of precast concrete." The business model of competing as an integrated design-manufacture-construct company offering more value and less risk per dollar invested in a new building was the route to that vision. Today, the company continues to redefine project delivery across multiple markets, making Finfrock D-M-Cs precast solutions the market leader. (Step 6 presents the leadership team's role in defining the vision, purpose, and guiding principles of the organization.)

A new idea for your business model, coupled with a new vision, will revitalize the management team. Team members can begin to look at the new big picture rather than continuing to try to preserve their own individual power. A true team spirit can take wing. As a result, the leadership team is able to look at the inherent weaknesses in its traditional approaches to business and to develop innovative ways to not only overcome them but also create a strategically differentiated business model.

In an environment of openness and cooperation, a team can realize that breaking down traditional barriers will give the company control of its own destiny. It will also retain or create strong operational management that not only generates profits but ultimately contributes to advancing or creating differentiation.

Focus the CEO on Increasing the Leadership Capacity of the Senior Leadership Team and Its Members versus Making Team Decisions

Collaboration doesn't just happen because some members of the leadership team realize that the concept is a positive thing. The limits of the leadership team's effectiveness are defined by the CEO's ability to grow and mature as a collaborative leader.

The only behavior the CEO can ultimately control is his own behavior. Therefore, we cannot emphasize enough the importance for the CEO of any company (or general manager of any business unit) to grow in maturity as a leader. Such maturity directly impacts the leadership team's capacity to grow in effectiveness and better positions the company to win.

Building a collaborative leadership team does not negate the need for a strong CEO, however. There are three key roles for the CEO in the transformation of any company.

1. *Creating an effective and positive corporate culture.* The CEO sets the corporate culture of the organization—the values and norms the company will follow in making decisions and working together. One of the most important things the CEO can do is articulate the desired culture to others in the organization.

2. *Ensuring that direction and priorities are set and that operating mechanisms are in place to track progress, and to intervene early when intervention is called for.* The CEO's energy is also vital for creating an organization that has a shared vision of where (and why) it is going, and how it will get there.

3. *Building the right leadership team.* The CEO must decide if the right people are on board. In companies undergoing a significant change process to break out of commodity competition, changing the players sometimes becomes necessary. A collaborative approach will not be possible without the right people. Conflict and disagreement are important in the leadership team, but once a decision is made, the team must act as one. Individuals who bring dissension into the company after team decisions

are made will destroy any efforts to build a collaborative culture in the organization because their actions reduce trust. Leadership starts at the top, and the uncomfortable job of dismissing leaders who are unwilling to work as a member of a collaborative leadership team rests with the CEO. On a more positive note, the CEO also plays a vital role in developing the potential of the individual leaders who are, as Jim Collins notes in *Good to Great*, on the bus.[13] In the case of Finfrock D-M-C, Robert needed to replace some of the members of the leadership team to initiate the transformation of his company.

At the beginning, before the entire leadership team is on board, the CEO's commitment is essential. As a collaborative leadership team is built, there is less and less need for the CEO to be the driver of change. With a collaborative culture, the CEO's role focuses upon coaching the leadership team, both individually and as a group, as well as doing the work that he or she can best do. This includes:

- Defining acquisitions strategy and leading or overseeing its execution
- Establishing or enriching vital industry and community partnerships
- Establishing and communicating core values of the organization
- Continuing to oversee culture change in the leadership team and organization
- Working with the outside board and investors and community stakeholders

Once the leadership team has fully stepped into its guidance role, more responsibility can be assigned to the next level of management—a group that should be eager to step up to the plate and take on more responsibility. Leaders won't give up work until they have more important work on their plate, which is why empowerment starts in the senior team.

As everyone's leadership skills are fully developed, the organization has much more potential to achieve success in its marketplace. The process will not be linear—no change process is. There will be ups and downs, victories and disappointments, and lots of learning. But the transformation becomes evident, and the company becomes extremely proactive in creating its desired future.

Some of the issues that arise in the transformation will result from a lack of experience. No change framework will compensate for lack of management experience and talent in making and executing decisions. But the ability of strong managers to succeed, absent a leadership team charter redefining their role and a collaborative culture, is very slight indeed.

Develop New Norms for the Leadership Team's Behavior, Documented in a New Leadership Team Charter

Nothing forces an issue as quickly as having to put the issue and its resolution down in words. Nothing assures a common understanding like having people agree on a written statement. These are two reasons why we've found that having a leadership team write a new charter for itself speeds up the shift to the new behaviors that are better aligned with the requirements of a newly defined business model.

A *leadership team charter* captures the unique aim and value that a leadership team brings to its organization. In many ways, a charter is like a job description, except that the focus is on what a *group* does, rather than what an individual does. The charter clarifies why members of a group meet together, and what comes out of their working together—in other words, the value added of their joint action.

Developing an effective leadership team charter helps leaders understand how a leadership team adds the most value to the organization. It focuses the team on the work only they can do—designing a strategically differentiated business model and overseeing its construction and enhancement. By changing how the team thinks of its role, you change its focus.

There are two other things a leadership team charter accomplishes.

1. *It serves as a benchmark for measuring whether certain individuals are qualified or properly motivated to be on the team at all.* For your team to succeed, you need the right players with the right attitude at the right positions. No matter how valuable players have been in the past, if they are not fully committed to the new charter and the change in thinking that it

demands, they no longer effectively contribute to the ultimate success of the team and should pursue their options elsewhere.

2. *By promoting the leadership team to more strategic work, it raises the performance expectations for managers reporting to them.* This shifting of responsibility is what gives the leaders the time to do the strategic work.

Crafting an effective leadership team charter will give you a solid foundation for making key team development decisions and business decisions that will set the company on a path toward strategic differentiation.

The charter should document the following:

- *The responsibilities you agree to take on as a team.* These will probably include those responsibilities outlined on page 137.

- *Decision-making procedures the team agrees to use.* These will address the following questions:
    - What types of decisions do individual members own with or without consultation with others?
    - What decisions must be made by the leadership team collaboratively?
    - How will a decision be made if a collaborative decision cannot be reached?

- *What parts of the business should be represented on the team.*

- *Specific norms or protocols for behavior within the team, acceptance of which is required as a condition of membership.* Norms are what others would see and hear if watching a videotape of the leadership team in action.

- *A description of the relationship between the team and others within the organization.* Companies will identify other core cross-department teams that convene that involve more than one member of the leadership team (e.g., category reviews, quarterly financial reviews, etc., that usually involve the larger management team).

- *Knowledge and skills that some or all members of the team must possess.* In addition to functional skills, leaders must develop key skills to contribute to the senior team. Although not all members need to be equally skilled at all skills, the charter should lay out the combination of skills that are represented around the table and those few skills that all leaders must have to remain at the table.

You are likely to want to see an example of a charter, but this is one time when examples can pull you away from the best result. There is no right or wrong approach. Some are wordy. Others are bullet points. Business units have extensive areas for collaborative decision making. The leadership team of a multi-business-unit organization will have far fewer areas for collaboration. *The process of creating the charter from a blank sheet of paper is the start of the leadership team change process.*

Lead Your Team through the Refocusing Process

Many leadership teams are operationally focused on the short term and are unaware of their primary role of leading the company out of commodity competition. The CEO or general manager is expected to decide on strategy that the direct reports will execute. Although the CEO typically seeks feedback in making decisions and tries to build consensus, other leaders often become yes-people or fail to be fully open about the reality facing the company. Each direct report often sees his or her role as ensuring the success of his or her part of the organization.

The discussion about where leadership teams add value to the organization can therefore be eye-opening. Some leaders will embrace the opportunity to delegate more of their day-to-day operational responsibilities. Others will resist delegation for a variety of reasons, which may include the following:

- If leaders already feel buried, the notion that they must do still more to fulfill their strategic leadership role will meet with great resistance. They will say, "But who will handle . . . ?" or "Our variances will be out of control," or "Our people are already overwhelmed. I can't throw anything more at them and I can't do what you're expecting me to do without unloading some of my work." This attitude can exist even in the CEO.

- If one or more members of the leadership team continue to push to redefine the role of the team, others may try to convince them that the company is really in better shape than it is and that the new business model is too risky or that change is not necessary.

- If leaders fear that they do not know how to fulfill their strategic leadership role, they will advocate only for incremental change. They know how to perform current roles quite well. Changing their role—to incorporate building a new business model and changing culture—raises too many fears.

How do you overcome this resistance to change? You must help leaders understand that your company is in the hands of its competitors and marketplace dynamics if the leadership team is not fulfilling its role in setting long-term direction and leading the transformation of the company.

You must redefine leadership: it is a duty and responsibility, not a reward for prior success; nor is it about getting paid more; nor is it a badge of honor. If leaders do not want first and foremost to be in service to others (versus command others), they should step aside for those who do want to serve.

If there are significant distrust issues in the team, you may need to spend time unraveling the root causes of distrust. Without a strong human resource function, organizational development consultants become necessary. They bring voice to a silence that hurts performance.

Finally, if you lack strong senior leadership team members, you may need to replace some members of the team or add a new leadership position before you can genuinely complete the work of this chapter. Individuals who are in the game only for themselves—with no consideration for peers or associates—will never become strong strategic leaders.

Conclusion

In the absence of a formal charter, members of the leadership team get pulled into day-to-day work they feel more secure managing. That's typical of the survival thinking to which commodity markets give rise.

Creating a charter for the leadership team provides a picture or vision of the type of shift the leadership team needs to make to move from operational management to strategic leadership. The charter is a living document that may evolve as the team matures. It provides a reference to regularly ask the question, "Are we as a team doing what we are uniquely positioned to do?"

However, creating a charter for your leadership team is just a first step. To ensure success, you will need to involve the entire company in executing the new strategically differentiated business model and get everyone invested in the new direction. It's a much more complicated issue than simply creating buy-in, as we'll discuss in the next chapter.

STEP 5 KEY POINTS

Realign the leadership team.

Desired goals:

- ✔ Commit as a leadership team to write a leadership team charter.

- ✔ Understand that the leadership team will need to work in a new way to create a strategically differentiated business model and to help the company grow more rapidly and profitably.

Keys to success:

- ✔ Do not be defensive. The past is past; there is no need to defend it.

- ✔ Think about what leadership really is and why it is so vital. Read books about and by leaders in business and other fields.

- ✔ Recognize that giving up individual power can build a more powerful organization within which your overall responsibilities and success will be greater.

- ✔ Openness. A team will have to understand and then forgive a lot of things that happened in the past that reduced trust and collaboration. They must understand how distrust arose from false assumptions about each other's motives and how openness can prevent future distrust from arising.

We can't solve problems by using the same kind of thinking we used when we created them.—Albert Einstein

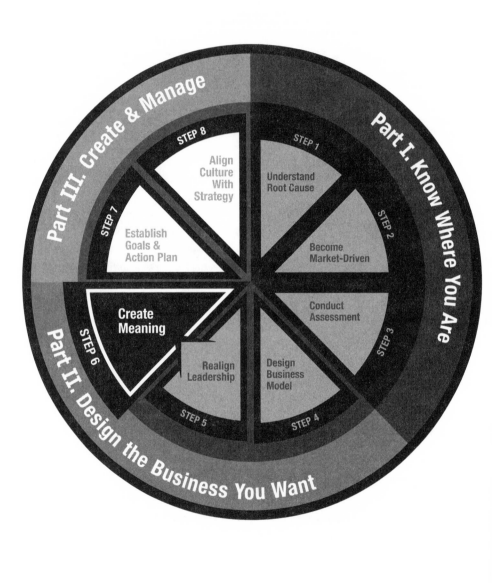

Step 6

Create a Meaningful Corporate Aspiration

A strategy without commitment is just words on paper.

Although Jay's human resource staffing company was growing at double-digit rates, he did not feel secure about the future. Consolidation in his industry had created large nationally located companies that could help national employers far better than Jay could help the offices located in the one region his business served. Jay didn't want to sell out to the consolidating publicly traded companies that were aggressively acquiring companies like Jay's. At the same time, he was concerned about future revenue streams, as potential clients in his region with national headquarters elsewhere were being forced by their headquarters to use contractual agreements with the national and increasingly international companies.

The only solution was a niche strategy—to serve the local and regional employers who did not necessarily need the nationwide or global services of the industry giants. Jay's team knew the company had to offer more than temporary help services, the core of Jay's business. The industry giants had a lower-cost structure for placing temporary help and, if they wanted to, they could easily attack Jay's niche position using lower prices.

Jay and his team set their vision as becoming local and regional employers' right-hand resource for human resource needs. They also defined this relationship so that Jay's employees would understand the level of collaboration, connection, and service his company would provide to its customers. Employees broadly discussed the vision, which led to three significant changes in the business.

1. The company dramatically expanded its offerings into a host of additional human resource services, from consulting to executive placement to human resource management outsourcing.

2. The company realized it would need to truly understand its business customers' culture, so that the people it sent to them for temporary or permanent positions were a good fit.

3. Independent service groups in the company would need to work collaboratively.

Furthermore, Jay's company would need to be very flexible so that employees would work with clients in ways that delighted clients. Jay was confident that the industry giants that prided themselves on operating efficiency would not be able to be as flexible as his smaller firm.

Jay's guiding principles—the core values by which the company did its work—did not change as the team went through the visioning process. Integrity, openness, going the extra step, and community service continued as their guiding principles.

But the new vision also led the company to reexamine its purpose. Leaders realized that their business was, at its core, dedicated to advancing the success of their customers and, through this, the success of the communities where Jay's business was located. Already Jay and his people were involved in many volunteer activities. Now, there was a clearer and shared purpose behind this involvement. The company began to identify ways it could advance its purpose by using the core skills of the company. For example, the company worked with Goodwill to place its sheltered workshop graduates (who all had work limitations) into for-profit companies. This service allowed Goodwill to help other disabled workers get training and helped Jay's customers address shortages of entry-level pro-duction workers. Jay also helped the local public university place spouses of potential faculty hires in jobs—increasing the success rate of the univer-sity in attracting top talent to its faculty. The inspiring purpose—making the community stronger—helped Jay more easily attract younger people to work in his company as the company's vision—being the right hand—ensured a client-focused culture. Both contributed to Jay's company's con-tinued success.

A new strategically differentiated business model presents your organization with a different and vastly improved way of doing business. Building a company that stays out of commodity market quicksand will require more than this, how-ever. What helps is having an overall aspiration—a clear description of what you are trying to create and why you are creating it—which will become the focal point that keeps your organization doing the hard work of reinventing itself.

NEVER FORGET

A business model is merely a means—a strategy. It exists in pursuit of a greater end—your corporate aspiration.

To understand the power of a shared and meaningful corporate aspira-tion, it's important to understand what people desire and what leaders can and can't directly manage. People desire meaning in their jobs—and rightfully so, given the amount of time they spend working and the opportunity cost of this time for their personal goals and responsibilities. Corporate aspirations create a means for employees to find meaning in their employment.

Furthermore, the inherent complexity of human interactions creates practi-cal limitations on the ability to completely manage the actions of others. Cor-porate aspirations, as with strategic positioning, extend management's ability to focus employees' actions in the same direction. Companies succeed by encour-aging, empowering, recognizing, and rewarding individuals as they help build a successful organization that achieves the company's aspirations.

A leader's role is not to make all the decisions and then demand that others do as they're told. Leaders cannot control actions to produce success along a planned route. Markets, customers, and competitors are too uncertain and complex for that leadership style to work. Rather, leaders should define a great design for their organization so that self-initiated efforts of others are aligned. They then create and preserve a rich environment in which individuals achieve their full potential, and team members work effectively alone and collectively. Leaders who empower others to do their best individually and as team members build the power of the organization while creating the framework in which to attain the desired future. As stated in the previous step, the more power you give away, the more powerful the organization.

Building an empowered environment starts by defining an effective aspiration—effective because it is shared and meaningful to the members of the company. *An organization's aspiration and its strategically differentiated business model are its essential design parameters.* They establish what the organization is trying to accomplish and the core strategic choices it will make to get there.

An aspiration gives the organization a sense of its future only if it is well defined and builds commitment. That means addressing these three elements which define the company stakeholders' intentions:

1. The purpose—why the organization exists

2. The guiding principles—a few key values, more important than profitability, that set boundaries on how the organization will fulfill its purpose

3. The vision—what the organization views as its desired future, stated as a long-term and inspiring outcome

Let's look at effectiveness in the context of each element of a corporate aspiration.

YOU ARE HERE

Link to previous steps: By completing steps 1 through 5, the leadership team now has a working theory of the best business model to use to pull the company out of and keep it out of commodity markets and survival mode mentality. Leaders also understand and accept the leadership team's role in the transformation. The model will become an accurate description of your company—however, only if people feel passionate about what the company can be. The proposed business model from Step 4 opens minds to new possibilities. This step broadens the view of the future in ways that evoke excitement within the entire organization so that your associates bring their full energy and attention to creating desired changes.

Expected outcome: A confirmation, redefinition, or deepening of the corporate aspiration, which consists of the organization's purpose, guiding principles, and vision. You will also create a written strategic framework that describes in detail the organization's direction.

Who is involved: The leadership team designs and facilitates the work of Step 6. Creating content for the aspiration is, nevertheless, a highly inclusive activity. The final writing and communication will be left to the leadership team.

Why this step is important: Although a new strategically differentiated business model is a necessary element for breaking out of commodity competition,

THE *BEYOND PRICE* PROCESS

The organization's purpose and vision act as reverse gravity.
They pull leaders and associates forward versus letting
them fall back into commodity competition.

it is unlikely to be sufficient alone. The work in this step supplies this missing link by creating enthusiasm for doing business in a new way. This enthusiasm is at the heart of building momentum to construct a business that reflects the new business model.

Defining Purpose

The *purpose* of the organization is a statement about why the organization exists. There are three things to understand about why purpose is so critical to your company and its change process.

1. Purpose states what you are bringing to others, not what your business is doing for you.

2. Purpose can be a constant source of motivation.

3. Purpose, when clearly defined by the company, better enables employees to link their life's purpose with your company's so that succeeding at work and succeeding in life are not in conflict.

In fact, purpose is more important than vision. Why? Because you can't create a shared destination or vision with others until you agree on the reasons for the journey. Purpose drives vision.

A good purpose statement has the following characteristics:

- It is meaningful to everyone. Individuals feel the purpose is in harmony with their own purpose.

- Customer and employee elements are included.

- It conveys a sense of destiny, uniqueness, and what would be lost if the organization ceased to exist.

- It is definitely not a generic statement that could apply to any company. Nor is it an eight-line hodgepodge of everyone's ideas.

Examples of Purpose Statements[14]

- Our real business is solving problems. *3M*

- The company exists to alleviate pain and disease. *Johnson & Johnson*

- Make people away from home feel that they're among friends and really wanted. *Marriott*

- We are in the business of preserving and improving human life. All of our products and services must be measured by our success in achieving this goal. *Merck*

- The company exists to honorably serve the community by providing products and services of superior quality at a fair price. *Motorola*

- Service to the customer above all else. *Nordstrom*

- To serve the most vulnerable. *Red Cross*

- We exist to provide value to our customers—to make their lives better via lower prices and great selection; all else is secondary. *Wal-Mart*

- To bring happiness to millions and to celebrate, nurture, and promulgate wholesome American values. *Walt Disney*

- To make computers for the rest of us. *Apple Computer*

- To fight hunger in our backyards. *Great Harvest Food Pantry*

- To make products people want to buy, enjoy driving, and will buy again. *Chrysler*

- To extend the years of being a girl versus a teenager. *Pleasant Company*

Identifying Guiding Principles

Guiding principles are the values the leaders and employees will follow as they do their work. There is no one set of "right" guiding principles; what is important is that they are acted on, as opposed to being window-dressing statements. Leadership must genuinely attempt to model the guiding principles through their own actions and words so that no cynicism develops around these principles. You know you have a strong guiding principle when people feel free at any time to say to any other employee, including a boss, "Your actions are not consistent with our agreed-to values."

Examples of Guiding Principles[15]

- Practice integrity in all that we do.
- All individuals are free to speak up about issues they see affecting the overall success of the organization.
- Our responsibility is not just to our customers, but also to our employees and the environment.
- We do what we say we'll do.
- The customer comes first.
- Treat all individuals with respect.
- Do something innovative every day.
- Demonstrate a commitment to personal growth and excellence.
- We reward people and teams who work collaboratively.

Describing Vision

The *vision* states what the organization ultimately hopes to accomplish. It's the destination—indeed the destiny—of the organization if its business model gets built and other strategies are executed. It provides direction, meaning, and focus. How do we know a good vision from a bad one? A good vision has the following characteristics:

- It provides a picture the audience can visually and emotionally feel—you will know it when you get there and you will know when you are still far away.
- It is understandable—people can explain it to their spouses.
- It is not outside the realm of possibility—although possibly a clear stretch and break from the past.
- It is inspirational and generates enthusiasm—the entire organization, not just the top managers, can get behind it.
- It encourages unified efforts toward a common good.
- It evolves from an understanding of the market (e.g., to be #1 in buggy whips fifteen years into the Ford era would not have been a good vision).

- It is far-reaching or enduring—albeit it evolves as the company evolves.

- It is unique.

Your vision should offer an opportunity for experiencing the vision in the present, although the percentage of your time with this experience is far less than you want. For example, you can be the number-one company with a small subset of consumers, but not yet the entire market. The experience of the vision is what creates energy to go after more of it more of the time.

Examples of Vision Statements[16]

- First in a new tier of packaging companies. *Placon*

- Beat Caterpillar. *Kamatsu*

- Quality is Job #1. *Ford*

- We made Wisconsin a world-class biotechnology center. Wisconsin Biotechnology and Medical Device Association

- Best experience for end users, our customers, and our employees. *Springs Window Fashions*

- Shaping our future as the solution of choice. *Precast/Prestressed Concrete Institute*

- We set the standards in our industry. *Wind River Financial*

Defining or Redefining Your Corporate Aspiration

The process we recommend for defining the organization's aspiration starts by having the leadership team share the new business model (and any elements of the aspiration the leadership team has discussed) with the whole company or in large companies with the entire management team followed by small groups of representative employees. The leadership team elicits feedback from employees, then takes what they've heard to either refine or adapt the model or aspiration as needed.

Subjecting your business model to the scrutiny of others and creating a shared and meaningful corporate aspiration builds the commitment you need to execute the new business model.

Many leaders feel this high-involvement approach is too time intensive. They feel it is better to make decisions as a leadership team and then "sell it" to everyone else to garner "buy-in." While the "sell-it" method may be faster, the overall execution of the strategy will be far slower than if you involve the whole organization from the beginning. People do not want to be changed, but they will gladly step into a change process that they are helping to define and execute.

The sell-it method yields compliance, at best. The difference between the enthusiasm of committed leaders and associates and that of compliant ones is like night and day. What attitude on the part of your workforce do you want showing up for work—commitment or compliance?

Start the process off by gathering all managers and employees, in total or in smaller groups, and have leadership team members share what has been learned about the need for change and the new business model that they feel will create greater success for the company. (Do not have individual leaders talk only to their own departments. The leadership team must show up as a team.) Talking about the business model first will open others' eyes to the possibility of doing business in a new way. This view unlocks the possibility of new corporate aspirations.

In the meeting(s), be sure to explain how you decided on the business model and then open the conversation to questions and comments. Often, small group breakouts build stronger involvement and more creative thinking. Have your leaders facilitate these groups, as the exchange with others is vital to understanding employees' reactions. No breakout group's report is as rich as the breakout group conversation.

Ask each group the following questions about the new business model:

- What questions do you have?
- What, if anything, is consistent or inconsistent with how we work today?
- What existing customers/clients and products and services best fit the new business model?
- What new customers/clients and products and services might this point toward?
- Does this business model provide needed focus to where we will grow and how we will win new customers, clients, or consumers?
- What positives do you see coming from this change?
- What negatives or uncertainties do you see coming from this change?
- Any other comments?

The leadership team must be open to hearing what employees have to say. Leadership's job is not to defend the recommended business model but to listen in ways that help make the new business model and its execution stronger. Clarify any misunderstandings. When people have great ideas for strengthening or broadening the model, compliment them.

Many organizations already have an aspiration—purpose, guiding principles, and vision of the company. If so, present these again to the employees and ask:

- Are our purpose and vision meaningful to you? If not, why not? Does our purpose capture what would be lost if our business did not exist?

- Are our guiding principles consistent with how we really behave? What are the disconnects?

- With our new business model, should our purpose and vision be expanded or made more specific?

- What guiding principles must we retain if we are to move forward together effectively?

The leadership team should then take these ideas and revise or create a draft statement of purpose, guiding principles, and vision. This corporate aspiration should then be shared across the company to assess whether it passes the test for employee understanding and commitment. (Remember that people change at different paces. Do not be disappointed that some coworkers have a wait-and-see attitude. Often, these people become the best champions of the change process as they subject the new ideas to careful scrutiny. If they are informal leaders, their delay and then acceptance communicate strong belief in the new direction.)

After the aspiration is well defined and accepted, the business model should then be revised to be in accord with it and the employee input received. Both the aspiration and the business model should then be presented to the employees as the business's strategic framework. If the Step 6 process is conducted all along to advance listening, the end result should be enthusiastic acceptance by employees of the corporate aspiration and strategically differentiated business model.

Having completed this work and earlier steps, you now have the foundation for your business's strategic framework.

ASPIRATIONS CAN CHANGE . . . BUT SLOWLY!

Going forward, be sure to treat the corporate aspiration as a living document. Look at it regularly and ask, "Are we true to our aspiration? If not, why not?"

However, an aspiration that is constantly changing focus may not have been well conceived. Company employees often criticize their leadership for changing the game plan. The feeling that things are constantly changing erodes employees' confidence in leadership. Although annual plans—how and to what ends resources are deployed in the fiscal year—will change, the changes should be made within a framework that stays relatively constant year to year. Your aspiration and business model are far more constant than annual activity. So are strategic goals, which will be discussed in Step 7.

Constant change indicates a failure of the leadership team to be properly aligned and focused in the same direction. If you find yourself constantly needing to modify any aspect of the aspiration or business model, it may be time to take a step back with your leadership team and reassess before moving forward.

CREATING AN ASPIRATION WHEN ONE DOES NOT EXIST

If your organization lacks a statement of aspiration, ask each participant to select at least one question from each section (purpose, guiding principles, and vision) and spend twenty minutes writing answers to these questions. Then break into small discussion groups and have each person share his or her ideas with the group, allowing about an hour for the whole group discussion. The small groups should record all the ideas that are discussed and appoint a spokesperson to present them to the larger group.

Questions Related to Purpose

- If our company ceased to exist, what would be lost? By whom?
- Why is it important for our company to continue to exist?
- Why did our founder create this company?
- What are we most proud of?
- What could this company do to make me continue working here even if I won the lottery?

- What one thing could we do, on which it would be worth focusing the rest of our working lives, even if we did not fully succeed?

- Employees commit to our organization a large amount of their valuable time. What does this company bring to the world that warrants this level of commitment?

- What could we do that would attract the best talent in our industry?

Questions Related to Guiding Principles

- If we wanted to recreate the very best attributes of our organization's culture elsewhere, which five to ten people would we select from our organization to accomplish this? What is it about these people, and how they work with others, that led us to select them?

- From what principles should we never depart—even if business conditions significantly change?

- The president of a manufacturing company once wrote, "What we want is for every person in our organization to uphold the norms of behavior or rules that, if followed, could replicate the whole organization and its success elsewhere." What do we want our company norms of behavior or rules to be? When we hire people, what values and personality attributes must they hold to signal they will be able to work well in our culture?

- If our company was to start in a new line of work, what guiding principles would we want to retain?

Questions Related to Vision

- Imagine that you are delivering a retirement speech. What do you want to say about your company's success and why it makes you proud?

- If a dream could be realized, what would be yours for your company?

- What is your vision for the end of your career? What do you want to have personally accomplished?

- If your company achieved all of which it is capable, what would it have accomplished?

- What kind of ultimate contribution or achievement would you want the company to make—more than just being the best in its industry, very profitable, and a great place to work?

- Consider the following brief excerpt from an interview with author Joe Jaworski of *Fast Company* magazine[17]:

  Q: In business, what is the job of the leader?

  A: Leadership is discovering the company's destiny and having the courage to follow it.

  Q: Do you believe that companies have destinies?

  A: Yes, I do. A company's destiny is a matter of purpose, an expression of why it exists. I think we're beginning to understand that companies that endure have noble purposes.

- Ask yourself, "What would I want the 'destiny' of our company to be?"

Pulling the Pieces Together: Your Organization's Strategic Framework

Your company's strategic framework summarizes the work the leadership team has done thus far. It consists of the following:

- The purpose of your organization
- Guiding principles to guide how work is done and decisions are made
- Your vision for your business
- The strategically differentiated business model:
  - Your target market(s) and situations
  - Business you are in
  - Your value promise—why you are selected over the alternatives
  - What you must do right to fulfill your value promise in ways competitors cannot easily copy

Some leadership teams take the strategic framework even further to define items such as:

- The types of employees they will hire and promote
- Their approach to management
- What leadership expects of employees and what employees can expect of leaders
- The basis of rewards
- Key business practices
- The one key shift in their culture they are trying to make (This will be covered in Step 8.)

In other words, the strategic framework becomes a detailed description of the company that the leaders are trying to create. Share it broadly.

The strategic framework becomes like our country's Declaration of Independence and Bill of Rights—it defines what is being created and why. Like our nation's founders, effective decisions at the start can build an enduring success. Over time, the business model may be revised. With successes attained, the vision must be extended to become even more far-reaching. But much of the organization's strategic framework will remain constant from year to year.

Leading Toward the Aspiration

As with the other steps in this process, you will encounter resistance here, especially if your company has had lots of failed change efforts. Others may want to label this new work as yet another "flavor of the day" initiative. Fear of not getting the day-to-day work done will be especially heightened at this stage. People—both senior leaders and others—will argue that the company is too busy to do today's work *and* engage in change.

If there have been other failed change efforts, underscore what is now different. You now have a new strategically differentiated business model, and the leadership team knows that change starts with them.

It is vital that leaders create the right teams throughout the company. Replace leaders who want unchallenging, weaker people under them. These types of leaders are lethal to a successful change effort because the demands of their own area will keep them from being an effective member of the leadership team. Replace these weak leaders with talent that brings new skills into the organization and a can-do attitude and energy level that will accelerate your change process. While we appreciate that our advice sounds cold, we are advising what is ultimately in the best interests of the largest group of coworkers. Before making any changes, be sure you give leaders the training and opportunities they need to succeed.

You must not allow this new business model to become a second business to run *if* people have time left after running the original business. You must help people understand that they must use their day-to-day work to create the change you and they want. Step Seven helps to make this possible.

Share examples of other companies that have broken out of and remained out of commodity competition. If possible, send a team, which represents a cross section of your company, to visit them.

Conclusion

Max DePree, CEO of Herman Miller and a noted leadership expert, comments: "All choices come with ready-made consequences. The real danger lies in blind complacency. Not to see our choices may be worse than making poor decisions. Be alive to the alternatives."[18]

Think of your company as the masterpiece of a talented artist. The organization you build is your easel. Your leadership skills are your palette. Your efforts, if sincere, are as special as those of your favorite painter or screenwriter or composer. Just as her art moves your heart, your efforts as a leader can inspire your people to achieve more—individually and collectively. Although inspiring others is hard work, it is among the most important things you'll ever do. Your efforts help to make the lives of your coworkers more meaningful. What work could be more important?

You've just completed a lot of work representing new choices about where your company is headed. The consequence in raising aspirations is that people will expect to see you back the new aspiration with execution. If the aspiration is meaningful and they trust you and feel you are competent, they will follow you into executing that aspiration.

Even though you have completed the very important work of creating your corporate aspiration, you must regularly ask yourself and other leaders the following questions:

- What are we trying to create?
- What level of excellence and fulfillment do we want to create?
- What types of relationships do we want to see in our company?
- Which of my gifts am I trying to use and develop?
- What are our measures of true success for our business? Our people?
- What are my measures of success for my personal and professional roles?

The question your leadership team must ask of its employees regularly is, "How are we doing, and what do we need to do differently?" This question is the subject of the next two steps.

STEP 6 KEY POINTS:

Build commitment and enthusiasm by creating a meaningful corporate aspiration.

Desired goals:

✔ Define aspiration—purpose, guiding principles, and vision.

✔ Create and share the business's strategic framework so that all may relate to what the company and its leaders are trying to create.

✔ Refine the strategically differentiated business model in accord with your corporate aspiration and employee input.

Keys to success:

✔ Be open to new ideas.

✔ Listen.

✔ Remember that no one person has all the answers.

✔ Forge a shared aspiration by enhancing communication between those with different ideas.

A strategy without commitment is just words on paper.

PART III

Create and Manage Your New Business

Be the change you want to create.

The first six steps of the *Beyond Price* framework helped you build a strong aspiration and a strategically differentiated new business model to achieve it. Now comes the hard work of making these decisions a reality.

Step 7: Establish strategic goals and create an annual planning process to achieve them.

Step 8: Align culture with strategy.

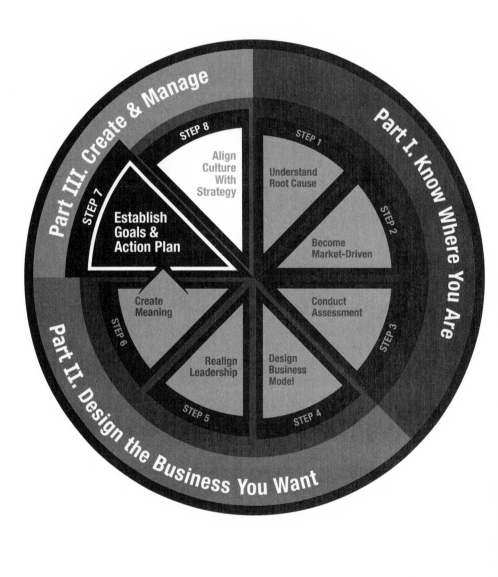

Step 7

Establish Strategic Goals and Create an Annual Planning Process to Achieve Them

Create differentiation in fact, not just on paper.

(This is a continuation of Step 5's story so that you can see how a newly focused leadership team worked to execute the new business model.) A national retailer of window fashions thinks of itself as being in the business of providing privacy, managing light, and enhancing room appearance. The company sells to two target markets: national retailers like The Home Depot and JCPenney, and designers and decorators working from an independent store, design studio, or their home.

The company has dramatically improved its performance since 2000 because it answered the four core strategy questions every leadership team must answer: "What business are you in?" "Who is your target market?" "What value promise will lead your target market to choose you?" and "Why can you deliver on your value promise better than your competition?"

In her role overseeing how work gets done, Debi, the VP of People, Process, and Culture, daily lives out the last question. "The heart of our company's competitive advantage is that we know how to deploy our people to fulfill our customer promise—to offer the Best Experience in our industry," Debi says.

This promise emerged from the company's strategic planning in 2000. Market research revealed that the company and its competitors regularly disappointed customers. The Best Experience promise offered an oasis in a category full of quality issues, delays, and other difficulties in selling, purchasing, and installing products. More than a phrase, the Best Experience promise was translated into a list of what they want customers and end users to say about the company and its products (e.g., "problems resolved in a snap," and "easy to order").

According to Debi, the Best Experience promise also created an execution platform for company associates. "Success is really about the performance system you create for your people," says Debi. "Telling people the direction you want them to go in and hoping they get there is not enough. Leaders must drive the deployment process so that people are doing the right things in the right ways—so that your internal culture, priorities, and focus align with what you want to create for customers. In our case, if customers were to have the Best Experience promise, our associates must also have the best experience."

Once leadership decided to win on a Best Experience promise, it looked to the rest of the organization to design how to create it. Says Debi, "Engaging our people in defining Best Experience got all our associates to understand what we were trying to do as a company. The act of discovery put meat on the bones of our strategy." For example, associates defined strategy from an action perspective, transforming Best Experience from a "what" to a "how" at a very strategic level. Best Experience enabled them to make everyone part of the business. "It created the platform for everyone's success," says Debi.

Under the Best Experience umbrella, the company dramatically enhanced its supply chain performance and adopted an innovation system. To ensure that this project-management system succeeded, multiple tools and on-the-job training experiences were developed to help people have successful experiences as a member, leader, or sponsor of a team. These tools helped the company create their deployment advantage.

Today, leadership is challenging teams to create even better experiences in both target markets. Internally? Even the company cafeteria caterer is being challenged to create better lunches. The company's response to a business necessity of moving work to Mexico and Asia was one of the most caring-about-and-for-people restructuring efforts previously witnessed in the community.

As a result of your work in earlier stages, you've defined the company you want to run—its aspiration and its strategic positioning. Your work now, as a leadership team, is to lead your associates, at all levels and places in the organization, to use their daily work to transform the company into what you want it to be. In essence, you are aligning everything to the new design.

YOU ARE HERE

Link to previous steps: Steps 1 through 6 created the design for the company the organization wants to run. The company's purpose, guiding principles, and vision (its aspiration) and the route to that vision (its strategically differentiated business model) are both in place. The question now becomes, "How do we start to run that business, versus the business we are now running—one that is stuck in or soon headed into commodity market quicksand?"

Expected outcome: The leadership team, with feedback from key managers and others, defines three-year strategic goals that, if achieved, will place the business well on the path to realizing its vision and transforming its business model. The leadership team will then involve managers and key personnel in an annual planning process that produces an annual business plan—a series of commitments and decisions that allocate financial and time resources in ways that will create significant progress against the strategic goals. The starting point for the annual business plan is leadership establishing what progress could be made in one year against the strategic goals, thereby defining the one-year goals for the business plan. These annual goals may be modified as detailed planning in six areas occurs. At the end, an annual business plan aligned to the strategic goals emerges, a plan that focuses and aligns all the activities of the organization. The activities in this step may also identify some one-time activities of the leadership team, e.g., restructuring or creating a better measurement system.

Who is involved: In moving from design to action, involvement moves from the leadership or more broadly defined management team out into the whole of the organization.

Why this step is important: Execution is where success happens or fails to happen. Although there may be two or three decent business models for a company, only one type of execution drops money to the bottom line—successful execution. As high as the stakes are, execution is where management's operational experience and skills finally come into play. Chances of success are high if you have a good management team with strong deployment skills.

You have two key tools at your disposal to transform your company so that it aligns with the new strategically differentiated business model. The first is *strategic goals* and the second is *annual planning* (or in really fast-moving industries, quarterly planning) to achieve these goals. Most businesses already have these elements in place, but they and the processes that created them must be revisited if you want to drive your company toward the new aspiration and effectively executing your new business model. In the discussion that follows, we give examples of typical ways in which strategic goals and annual plans need to change to support a new business model. Use these guidelines to help you evaluate and modify your own goals and plans.

Understanding Strategic Goals

An important step in making a new business model a reality is to identify the longer-term outcomes—which we'll call strategic goals—you hope to accomplish (such as a higher percentage of sales from new products, entrance into a new market, a shift from manufacturers' representatives to your own sales organization, or gains in revenue, profitability, or market share) and the changes your company needs to make in order to execute that new model (e.g., development of a strengthened or new skill). Defining strategic goals is important because having clearly stated strategic goals does these three things:

1. *The goals shift the organization out of a decision-making mode into action.* They define what the organization needs to accomplish within the next three years to move the new business model from concept to action and move closer to the vision. As such, they are overarching organizational outcomes the leadership team is committing the company to achieve. Accomplish them, and you will be much closer to your vision. They demonstrate that you're walking on the road to the new vision based on the new business model. As the stepping-stones to the vision, strategic goals engage associates at all levels and functions of the organization in action planning.

2. *Employees focus on the longer-term game plan.* Without that focus, associates inadvertently undermine future success in order to achieve immediate success. Annual goals, strategies, and objectives that are linked to strategic goals ensure that employees know what to do today to advance success not just this year but three years from now. Individuals are challenged to use this year's efforts to achieve a longer-term goal.

3. *All parts of the organization are aligned toward the same specific aim.* Strategic goals set the agenda for each part of the organization and each individual. Individuals will design specific objectives for themselves and their teams to ensure that the organization's strategic goals are met. It is an often forgotten principle of systems dynamics that *success depends on how well parts are aligned toward achievement of a shared aim, not how well each part performs in isolation.* Strategic goals create this alignment. For example, a sales force will not help create a winning company if its objectives are not aligned with those of the entire organization. A sales force that focuses on volume versus profit is a classic example of sales optimization at the expense of organizational success.

GOALS, STRATEGIES, AND OBJECTIVES

There is much debate about the terms *goals, strategies,* and *objectives.* In our vocabulary, goals are the final outcomes a group commits to. Strategies are how the group will achieve those outcomes/goals. And objectives are measurable deliverables that, if met, will collectively execute the strategies and achieve the goal. This distinction is vital. If managers fail to identify true strategies for achieving their goals, the annual business plan then becomes a statement of annual goals alone, with no clear direction for how these goals will be achieved. Maintaining the goal-strategy-objective framework forces managers to identify not just **what** they want to achieve but **how** they want to achieve it.

Defining Strategic Goals

Defining the right strategic goals is an art. It requires that you think logically, sequentially, and creatively about how to change the organization so as to be true to the new business model.

Well-written strategic goals have the following four properties:

1. You can determine whether or not they are achieved.

2. You can write strategies and objectives to achieve them.

3. They take the company beyond the next fiscal year.

4. They are organizational outcomes—not outcomes for one department alone that depend solely on that department's efforts. (For example, a change in a sales force distribution channel will require work on the part of marketing, finance, and sometimes manufacturing.)

Each strategic goal should capture a key area of change for the company. Strategic goals may, for example, be defined around overall revenue or profit growth, market share gains, new skills of the organization, a better work environment, or entering a new market. To identify these areas, engage the entire management team (or an even broader group if desired) in a brainstorming session that could be structured as follows:

1. Review the comments from the employee meetings in Step 6. These comments will refresh the management team's thinking about what needs to change.

2. Create small cross-functional breakout groups to discuss the questions "What must change around here to execute our new business model and achieve our vision?" and "What results will we hope to see to know our new business model is moving us toward our vision?" Have each group record its ideas.

3. Pool the findings of the different breakout groups to derive rich insights for the change agenda of the organization. You do this by taking the wealth of responses about what has to change and then clustering individual responses into groups representing similar types of changes. In all probability, each discussion group will return with strategic goals as well as strategies for achieving the strategic goals.

4. Have the leadership team then work with each cluster of ideas to arrive at a specific strategic goal statement and a set of potential strategies for achieving that strategic goal.

GOALS SHOULD BE INTERDEPENDENT BUT DISTINCT

The strategic goals will likely be interdependent because, collectively, they should move the organization toward its vision and execution of the new business model. Yet, at the same time, each strategic goal should describe a distinct outcome around which the organization can engage in action planning.

For example, revenue growth may be one goal and cost reduction another. Cost reduction helps create money to fund marketing efforts that help grow revenue. But the work that is done to pull costs out of a manufacturing system, for example, will be quite distinct from work to gain market share. Stating both goals reminds everyone that the company should not achieve one goal at the expense of another. Strategic goals carry this interdependency and therefore advance breakthrough thinking.

Articulating Typical Changes in Strategic Goals

Some likely areas of change around which strategic goals can be written include the following:

- Internal process changes
- Value chain redesign
- Product and service additions or redesigns
- Target market share increases
- Infrastructure or work environment changes
- Improved financial performance

THINK YOUR CURRENT STRATEGIC GOALS ARE OK?

If you do not feel there are any changes you need to make over the next three years, rethink whether you have the right business model. If you still feel you should stick with the same business model, there are undoubtedly ways you can enhance customer value and, without significant time or expense, create advantages competitors cannot easily copy.

Identify internal process changes.

A friend, Dave Boyer, once wisely observed in the midst of a major operational mess, "Every system is perfectly designed to get the results it gets." If you want a different set of results, if you want to do something of more value for your target market, you will need to do your work differently. Designing and operating key internal processes in new ways will further advance the creation of a core competency and therefore defendable differentiation.

Most companies already have clearly defined processes and process improvement goals. The question to ask now is whether you have designed your processes to build the differentiation defined in your new business model. For example, the window blind manufacturer featured in the opening story realized that with its new Best Experience value proposition, supply chain management and new product development would warrant far more investment than the company had made in the past. These two processes were far more strategic at this point in the company's history than the sales and marketing process. Improve them, while maintaining sales and marketing process excellence, and revenue would easily increase.

To create the distinction you desire, look first and foremost at how your processes are working, just as you would look to change features and benefits of a product if it were no longer differentiated. Entire books are written about how to do process improvement and process redesign. Therefore, it is not the intent of this book to teach process management. Rather, we will focus on how to approach process management in a way that aligns the organization to its value proposition.

WHY ARE PROCESSES VITAL?

There are at least three reasons for focusing on the processes at work in your company.

1. The organization is only as good as its underlying processes. Processes are how the organization does its work. They are at the heart of differentiated customer benefits and direct and indirect cost savings. Core competencies are a collection of processes and knowledge and their relationship to one another that enable the organization to offer compelling benefits that competitors cannot easily copy.

2. A process focus lets you eliminate problems versus treating their symptoms. You must look at any issue as a whole, that is, from a systems perspective. This is because it's the interaction of parts, not the parts themselves, that defines behavior and dictates outcomes in any system. If sales keeps on selling more than the capacity of operations, success will not be forthcoming. In fact, the recurring backlogs in an organization where sales oversells will set in motion reduced customer satisfaction that will eventually reduce the success of the selling organization.

3. A process focus creates an empowered organization. It focuses leaders on the work only leaders can do (i.e., improving the interactions among the different processes or departments and making sure processes are designed well). It is up to others—the line managers and workers—to actually do the operational

work. When leaders focus on their unique role as leaders, the rest of the company's productivity, morale, and creativity increase. This is especially important because a key strategic leadership practice is enabling others to do their best. Removing barriers that undermine people's ability to do their work—versus doing their work for them—creates credibility as a leader.

Focus on specific improvements and allocate needed resources.

Selecting processes to improve or redesign is at the heart of successful strategic leadership. All too often, process improvement resources are focused on processes that are not at the core of differentiation. That's because one of the mistakes the quality movement made at its start was to treat all processes as equally deserving of improvement. As a result, organizations "get better," but they don't necessarily create differentiation, which is the key to breaking out of commodity quicksand.

Although all processes can be improved, organizations have limited resources, so it is vital to focus improvement or redesign efforts on the key processes that, when successfully designed and managed, do the most to differentiate your company's offerings and secure a market leadership position. Those are your *critical processes*. They let you fulfill your firm's value proposition effectively and efficiently. They are at the heart of competitive advantage.

Critical processes

- Are few in number
- Are linked horizontally and vertically in your organization
- Can be diagrammed in terms of their interaction with other parts of the organization
- Can be measured (although not always easily)
- Can be improved through redesign or incremental improvement

After identifying critical processes, you must select those that require improvement or redesign. Specifically, determine which ones enhance or detract from creation of your strategically differentiated business model and attainment of your strategic goals.

What should you do about an underperforming process that is not a critical process? You should only improve or redesign the process if: (1) it is or will eventually become a customer requirement; (2) it could enhance your value or create differentiation in the customers' eyes; or (3) there is a realistic and attractive financial payback to improving the process.

EXAMPLES OF PROCESS CHANGE STRATEGIC GOALS

- *Strategic Goal:* Achieve 95 percent on-time delivery while cutting lead times in half. *Strategy:* Utilize supply chain make-buy decisions and process improvement redesign/improvement in process steps with largest bottlenecks.

- *Strategic Goal:* Create a stronger market understanding process. *Strategy:* Hire a market research leader and benchmark with leaders in other industries who have a strong market-understanding process.

- *Strategic Goal:* Build an advantage in ergonomic design. *Strategy:* Hire design talent and change our sales process to create time for design innovation.

- *Strategic Goal:* Design product platforms that will enable customization at the customer level for our three major categories. *Strategy:* Utilize customer input and seek lowest number of manufacturing parts.

- *Strategic Goal:* Move P&L management to first-line managers. *Strategy:* Adopt new evaluation and salary and benefits system.

Redesign your value chain.

Although process improvement and redesign are vitally important, you may need to change your value chain to truly deliver on your value proposition or to reach new target markets more effectively. Your company's value chain defines the way your organization relates to suppliers, partners, and channels to deliver value to your target market. If it needs to change, this change should be reflected in a strategic goal. (See Step 3 for a discussion of value chains.)

Companies often take their value chain as a given and never challenge whether it could enhance the value it delivers to customers. A new business model will often require a new channel strategy and a shift in what you seek from outside suppliers or what you are doing internally. For example, in seeking to improve its new product development process, the window blind manufacturer might have considered a strategic alliance with an outside design house, which would have been a change from its "everything invented here but the material" current practice. A critical strategic decision that leaders face therefore is to determine which activities the organization should do themselves versus which ones to outsource or to form strategic partnerships to complete.

Can you better execute your business model and improve your critical processes by bringing "steps" into your company? Finfrock D-M-C, in targeting the owner, had to move from a subcontractor business definition to being a design-build general contractor. It brought architectural and general contracting processes into its company. Interface (one of the first corporations to change its offering to not hurt the environment) differentiated itself by making its carpeting environmentally sustainable, or "green." This involved significant changes in its sourcing (a process change) and adding steps related to recovering carpeting at the end of its useful life (a value chain change).

Or, would you better execute your business model by having outside partners do work you once did because they are better at it? Through strategic alliances, organizations can marry their expertise, core competencies, products, and services to create value that is greater than either can provide independently. For example, the window blind manufacturer might want to use outside manufacturers and not just an outside product development resource to enable faster change in looks than internal development allows.

EXAMPLES OF VALUE CHAIN STRATEGIC GOALS

- *Strategic Goal:* Build a loyal supplier network that operates as a team. *Strategy:* Hold quarterly meetings as a network.

- *Strategic Goal:* Replace manufacturer representatives with direct selling while retaining market share. *Strategy:* Use retention incentive contracts for outside representatives and encourage small rep firms to merge with our company.

- *Strategic Goal:* Vertically integrate into design to incorporate the voice of the customer into our offering. *Strategy:* Hire outstanding design talent to incorporate more customer features in our offering.

Add or redesign products and services.

New and redesigned offerings are often the most important area of change for a company inaugurating a redefined business model. For example, in Step 4, a commercial sewing company's business model changed to its acting as a virtual subsidiary to the manufacturers of OEM branded marine equipment. This required many new services and a design competency, and creating these services became a key strategic goal of the organization.

You need to review your current offerings and ask: Do they reflect your new business model? Is the breadth of offerings optimized? Does your offering contain the features and benefits that are the evidence you will deliver on your value proposition? If not, you will need to translate your strategically differentiated value proposition into an offering that reflects it. Otherwise, your strategic framework might as well sit on the shelf, never to be referred to again.

Every organization should try to create a balanced new-products portfolio (that reflects its value proposition) to bring to the target market. You can think of the balanced portfolio as blending the different types of hits in a baseball game (singles, doubles, triples, and home runs) in the most productive combination. Companies need an effective combination of different hits in their new products portfolio.

The process of developing a balanced portfolio can be challenging for the leadership and management team. Demands for new product resources inevitably exceed available resources. Outsourcing development is an option for expanding resources. Even so, the organization is forced into a hard discussion of which products are most worthy of investment. The value of having a clearly defined, strategically differentiated business model is that it helps surface the criteria (in addition to risk and reward) for selecting one new product idea over another. Any new or enhanced offering that does not fit the new business model and value proposition should be removed from the portfolio unless there are compelling financial reasons for its staying there, such as pulling costs out of a commodity-like product in order to hold share and fund investments to advance the new business model.

One of the hardest issues your leadership team will struggle with in creating the new-products portfolio is deciding how much to continue to invest in the old business model (and old portfolio) versus the new business model. Since it's the old portfolio that is accountable for all your current revenue, obviously you can't simply switch entirely from one to the other at the drop of a hat. But the more you invest in products or services tied to your old model, the fewer resources you have for building your company's future.

Some useful principles for resolving the investment dilemma include:

- When you are uncertain, err on the side of the new model.

- Make sure all added resources and a significant percentage of your resources are focused on the new model in year one.

- Put your best people on the new model and make sure they are focused and freed from working on the old model.

EXAMPLES OF STRATEGIC GOALS PERTAINING TO PRODUCT AND SERVICE ADDITIONS OR REDESIGNS

- *Strategic Goal:* Achieve 20 percent of revenue from new products tailored to new target situations. *Strategy:* Outsource design to accelerate new product development.

- *Strategic Goal:* Enter the breakfast meals category with our brand, securing $100M in revenue. *Strategy:* Acquire niche company.

- *Strategic Goal:* Modify offering to achieve $50M in sales from independent retailers. *Strategy:* Form an alliance or acquire a company with a strong relationship and brand image with the independent retailers and a strong product offering for this channel.

Increase target market share.

Does your new business model require changes in, or expansion or refinement of, your target market or the channel for reaching it? If so, establishing clear outcome goals related to target markets, distribution channels, and market share is important for driving change through the company. For example, the window blind manufacturer realized that if it was to offer consumers the Best

Experience in the window coverings category, the company would need to do a better job in meeting the needs of consumers who work with independent stores and designers to fulfill window treatment needs. Improving market share in the independent channel became a key strategic goal for the company.

Marketing accounting (defined in Step 3) is a useful tool to revisit as you write strategic goals. Sales within each target market is a function of served market revenue, awareness rate, consideration rate, win rate, relative purchase rate, and relative selling price. Identify which variable is most important to drive up to secure improved revenue and market share and define a strategic goal around it.

EXAMPLES OF STRATEGIC GOALS RELATIVE TO TARGET MARKET SHARE INCREASES

- *Strategic Goal:* Increase big-box national retailer share of total revenue from 15 to 25 percent of revenue while growing revenue 8 percent. *Strategy:* Tailor our offering to big-box consumer needs and retail chains' own differentiation needs.

- *Strategic Goal:* Secure $5 million in revenue from direct-to-consumer Internet sales. *Strategy:* Partner with firm X.

- *Strategic Goal:* Increase average order value by 25 percent. *Strategy:* Bundle multiple offerings into a single well-priced offering that saves customers' time.

Change your work environment or infrastructure.

People create change, plans on paper do not. A more supportive infrastructure and work environment improvements become important goals as a result. If your business's guiding principles include "treat all people with respect" and "develop and deploy talent," you'll need a strategic goal linked to people or the infrastructure that supports them.

EXAMPLES OF STRATEGIC GOALS RELATIVE TO INFRASTRUCTURE OR WORK ENVIRONMENT

- *Strategic Goal*: Reward and align employees' efforts. *Strategy*: Create a profit sharing plan linked to EVA and strategic achievement of our other strategic goals.

- *Strategic Goal*: Create a worker-friendly, less stressful but more productive work environment. *Strategy*: Redesign headquarters to create more independent quiet workspaces and community/team space.

Pursue higher financial performance.

Leadership teams should establish three-year financial goals for the organization tied to indicators that will reflect whether the company is moving toward its new vision. These financial goals create the discipline to fulfill the other strategic goals in ways that retain or build profitability.

Key cost reduction activities will fall under the financial performance strategic goal. Achieving the cost reductions may require process improvement changes or process redesigns, in addition to those necessitated to fulfill the value proposition. Creating a higher-margin goal is often recommended with a new business model—if the new model is not increasing margins and profitability by helping you move away from commodity competition, either you are not executing the model or you have made the wrong business model strategy decisions in light of competition and marketplace trends.

EXAMPLES OF FINANCIAL STRATEGIC GOALS

- *Strategic Goal*: Grow revenue 20 percent per annum for the next three years. *Strategy*: Open an additional channel and two new categories.

- *Strategic Goal*: Increase gross margins by twelve points. *Strategy*: Differentiation and cost reduction.

- *Strategic Goal*: Achieve 18 percent return on investment. *Strategy*: Purchase new financial management system and outsource two nonstrategic business functions that require physical capital.

Set other strategic goals.

We've covered the common strategic goals that have to be added or changed when adapting to a new business model, but don't be limited or wed to the categories we've listed. There may be other more essential changes your company needs to make (such as in leadership development, building your core competency, or innovation capability) that may be critical to your new business model.

Achieving Strategic Goals through Business Planning

With your strategic goals set, it is time to engage in annual planning for how you will achieve those goals. Annual (or in rapidly moving organizations, quarterly) business planning is the discipline that enables the organization to achieve its strategic goals. A good business planning process does the following:

- It uses annual goals, strategies, and objectives as business planning tools—identifying to what your organization will commit resources in light of your long-term strategic goals.

- Annual goals are directly related to the three-year strategic goals.

- It is replicated at lower and lower levels within the company.

  - The annual company planning process is a subset of the corporate long-term strategic goals. The annual business unit or department planning process is a subset of the annual company planning process. Individual performance objectives are derived from the annual department plan objectives.

  - This alignment allows each individual within the organization to understand what his or her contribution is to attaining the company vision. If anyone in your organization does not understand his or her contribution, you are missing the opportunity for a more motivated and therefore energized and creative associate.

- It covers six areas: marketing, sales, operations, products and services, corporate citizenship, and finances.

SIX COMPONENTS OF A BASIC ANNUAL BUSINESS PLAN

Here are the six areas we consider essential in any annual business plan. Each plan is linked to those strategic goals pertinent to the plan's focus. So, for example, a marketing plan and a sales plan will focus on revenue and new product introductions that create revenue growth. Each plan will have specific objectives—outcomes—related to the strategic goals and action plans and time lines for achieving the stated outcomes.

1. A **marketing plan** addresses revenue, margin, and market share goals and objectives; priorities for proactive marketing and sales; required outcomes for targeted markets; and strategies to achieve the outcomes. It also outlines the strategies and tactics around communications that will be used to convince potential customers in each target market to purchase from you and what you will do to combat any major competition.

2. A **sales plan** breaks down the company's annual revenue goal into strategies and objectives for each target market, as outlined in the market plan and sales territories. For example, sales objectives (dollars and units) will be set for current customers and for trials and repeats by noncustomers. The company may set a higher average selling price objective as new products or services (based on the new business model) are rolled out.

3. An **operations plan** addresses this question: "What must we change in our operations to support the annual sales and marketing plans and achieve other companywide annual goals?" The operations plan establishes how capacity, resources, and the operations workforce will be aligned with the sales plan and with desired operational changes (process improvements, skill development, value chain changes) outlined in the strategic goals. The operations plan is to inside activities of the business what the marketing and sales plans are to external activities. It will direct cross-departmental teams' activities as they relate to cost reductions, new product development, process redesign or improvement, outsourcing, the addition of new skills, and other annual objectives.

4. A **products or services plan** outlines (a) which new or revised products or services the company will begin or continue developing or have ready for introduction during the next year, and (b) which existing products or services it will continue to invest in and (c) which will be discontinued (because they do not fit

in with the new business model). Whether new products enter the revenue budget or not, you must still account for the associated employees, incremental costs, and time. The products or services plan is also the place where the company decides what offerings are branded with the company brand or sub-brands.

5. A **corporate citizenship plan** is now a standard plan component because company image is becoming increasingly important in purchasers' decisions and talented professionals' employment choices. Not surprisingly, there is more and more public information available about a company's impact on the environment and the community. In today's environment, reputation can often be a differentiator, both with customers, creative workers, and the younger generations who are increasingly seeking work with companies who have strong corporate citizenship reputations.

6. A **financial plan**, which presents annual or two-year financial projections and objectives, is often the tool used to test whether resources are being effectively deployed to execute strategy. Individual departments are asked to create budgets consistent with achieving all five other plans. If the resources required do not yield the desired profitability, it's back to the drawing board to find alternative ways to execute strategy and achieve financial targets. The financial planning process also ensures that all departments understand the overall objectives of the organization and are budgeting accordingly. The process of linking strategy to financial plans does not create a more hectic budget process. If anything, it helps the process, as there is less bickering across departments on what is and is not a priority. While great business model thinking requires clean sheets of paper without any numbers, business planning is ultimately all about time and money allocations and careful calculations.

There is natural give-and-take among these six business plan components and the business's annual goals. For example, sales and marketing planning may suggest that the annual revenue goal can be increased, creating more investment funds for product development. As a result, the target for a "percentage of revenue from new products" annual goal can be raised. The overall focus of business planning then is to align strategic goals with annual goals, objectives, and action plans across all parts of the organization.

In summary, an effective annual planning process ensures the following:

- Annual goals relate directly to three-year strategic goals. If you achieve the annual goals, you are on track to achieve your strategic goals and vision.
- Strategies are well thought-out ways to achieve the annual goals—not just restatements of the annual goals.
- Departmental initiatives and resource deployment to achieve each annual goal are outlined.
- A series of quarterly milestones are identified in each of the six business plan components, which gives management guidance on what must be monitored to ensure that the business plan is being followed.
- Each of the six components of the business plan *works in alignment with all the others.* The plans are like an interlocking set of building blocks that together build a stronger foundation and create success. For example:
  - Are planned marketing activities designed to best help sales achieve its revenue goals?
  - Has the operations department allocated resources to support the balanced new-products portfolio?
  - Can the company achieve its profit plan given planned marketing expenses?
  - Will sales achieve its revenue goal if marketing must be cut back?

FIGURE 7.1 *A disciplined and aligned planning process*

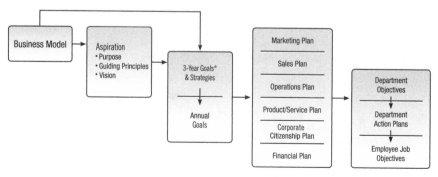

* Goals are defined for company or business unit and will require efforts across departments, or business units to achieve.

Checking Your Current Planning Process

Your company likely has its own planning process. Our intent here is not to supplant that process. Rather, here is a series of questions you can ask of your management team about its annual business plan to make sure it is an effective tool for executing your new business model:

- Are our annual goals linked to all the strategic goals or, instead, do they represent what we have to do to make this year's numbers, irrespective of changes demanded by the new business model?

- If we achieved our annual goals, would we be significantly closer to delivering on our desired value proposition? If not, what should we be doing to move in that direction?

- Do we have a goal or objective that ensures that we are maintaining and building the requisite core competency(ies) to deliver on our value proposition?

- Are our sales and marketing efforts focused on our strategic target markets? If not, why not? What market segments must we stop going after in order to become proactive in getting the business we want?

- Are we investing enough resources to change our offering? If not, will our new value proposition sound more like advertising spin than true differentiation? Do we have the right teams working on new product development?

- Has management winnowed down the list of new product initiatives to better focus our new product development teams and to ensure that we meet our deadlines? Has it advanced the right mix of potential home runs and surefire singles?

- Are we investing enough to create awareness around our new value proposition if we feel we are ready (i.e., we have enough evidence) to tell our story?

- Are there important market research goals that should be built into our plans? What don't we know that could really hurt or help us?

- Will the goals we set out to achieve this year set us up well to achieve our strategic goals within 3 years?

- Is our corporate citizenship plan a natural outgrowth of our purpose as a company? What are the synergies between our day-to-day work and what we are doing to enhance the well-being of our communities? Or, is our corporate citizenship about widely disbursed donations and giving coworkers some time off? What corporate citizenship activities or focus would be more synergistic with our core business?

- Is the financial plan realistic in these two ways: Are we forecasting revenues we can meet, and are we investing enough to execute the new business model?

TRANSLATE BUSINESS PLAN GOALS AND OBJECTIVES TO THE DEPARTMENT LEVEL

Remember, the goals and objectives of the company's annual business plan do not explain in detail what any one department will need to do for its part in achieving organizational outcomes. Therefore, after you have agreed on the organizational objectives, and the cross-functional teams have defined strategies for achieving assigned objectives (e.g., in marketing and sales plans), you need to create departmental plans to ensure that the organization's resource deployment will achieve the business's annual goals and objectives. So, for example, the marketing department's plan may include a major product pruning exercise, which will help manufacturing achieve its overhead cost-reduction objective. The departmental plan may also include an investors' communication plan, critical to the finance department's objective of preparing for taking the company public.

Identifying Typical Problems with Strategic Goals and Annual Plans

We see core issues associated with the planning process of companies slipping into or stuck in commodity competition. Our intention is to help you avoid these issues (see Table 7.1).

TABLE 7.1 *Troubleshooting the planning process*

PROBLEM	SOLUTION
Goals are too short term, or, if they are longer term, they are not linked to what is required to break out of or stay out of commodity markets.	Establish strategic goals—the key three-year milestones for executing your new strategically differentiated business model.
Annual goals are stated, but the organization lacks any cohesive, agreed-to plan for how they will be achieved.	Annual goals should contain or be accompanied by strategies for achieving them as well as detailed objectives against which the leadership team can monitor progress.
Annual goals come from the bottom up—making the organization's annual goals a sum total of what each department wants to achieve. This inevitably leads to silos whose work conflicts with other silos.	The annual goals should evolve directly from the vision, strategic goals, and new business model. They are shared commitments by all departments to which the departments will align their actions and measures over the next year. The six business plan components create that alignment.
The organization lacks a clear plan for where revenue growth will come from and the organizational (versus sales department alone) actions needed to deliver it.	Coordinated marketing and sales plans create a framework for deploying resources and investigating root causes if revenue falls short of budget.
There is no prioritization of new offerings. As a result, the organization is chasing too many new offerings with too few resources.	A balanced new-products portfolio is the solution. This requires a conscious set of decisions by the management team about what new and enhanced offerings will receive funding. These should positively stretch, but not overload, available resources.
Leaders fail to see how their corporate citizenship activities could be used to advance toward their vision and enhance their differentiation. As a result, citizenship becomes feel-good, publicity-related activities rather than a key strategy that reflects the company's broader purpose and its desired value proposition to the target market or employees.	Align corporate citizenship agendas with the company's aspiration, strategic goals, and business model. The net result is more beneficial for the company and the community. Ideally, work conducted for profits and work conducted to help the community are highly synergistic.

Pursuing Other Changes That Enhance Achievement of Strategic Goals

Although the annual plans will go a long way toward achievement of the annual and strategic goals, there are other directions a leadership team can pursue to ensure that the organization achieves its vision and executes its new business model. Here are five ways to enhance achievement of strategic goals:

1. Change incentives and performance measurement.
2. Adopt a continuous improvement philosophy.
3. Change the organizational structure.
4. Expand measures of success for the organization.
5. Let go of business.

Change incentives and performance measurement.

Incentives and performance measurement should be developed to align with your competitive strategy. Great care should be taken in developing your incentive and measurement programs, as that which receives incentives and is measured *will* be accomplished. It can be especially important to pay the sales force on margin, not revenue, to break the sales force habit of selling on price.

Adopt a continuous improvement philosophy.

Some leadership teams encourage their company to adopt what is called a *continuous improvement philosophy.* When it is in place, every process in the organization is measured, and improvements are made on a regular basis. The fundamental concept behind continuous improvement is that it is for the benefit of the customer. The focus is on both internal as well as external customers.

The philosophy of continuous improvement offers several advantages.

- Outputs of high value are produced when performance is measured.

- Teamwork is improved when everyone is involved in improvement.

- Organizations think in new ways when leaders develop systems thinking skills.

- A systems view replaces a focus on blaming individuals for problems with a desire to continually discover new ways to improve the organization for the benefit of customers.

Change the organizational structure.

Designing an organization chart is one of the strongest leverage points for aligning the organization to fit its new differentiated business model. It is a critical step to creating culture change and for getting people to focus on the right kind of work, performing to the right set of measures.

Therefore, after your strategy is designed and you understand the critical processes of your organization and its strategic goals, start with a blank sheet of paper and design the ideal organizational structure. Do not think at this stage about where people will fit. All that can come later.

An auto sensor company changed its business model to add the industrial market as a new target to its existing auto market. In fact, the goal of the new target market was to exit the auto market over time. Until the CEO created a stand-alone team, it was next to impossible for associates to steal time from a demanding market to work on initiatives for the new market with unsure revenue outcomes.

Many companies with a continuous improvement philosophy organize their company by process teams instead of functions. This shift can be instrumental in creating more effective processes, as the new structure changes relationships and therefore culture. Nevertheless, changing organizational structure alone is not sufficient for creating strong processes. People also have to be willing to work collaboratively to make the processes work well.

A useful way to think about structure is to ask, "Should we design around the critical processes of the organization?" For example, a simple structure might look like this:

1. Create the offering.

2. Secure and retain customers.

3. Support the other two teams.

An organizational structure that parallels the critical processes of the business is often easier to run than a structure defined by function. Nevertheless, this is a huge change in a company that has a silo culture. People in such cultures do not think laterally. If this is the case in your company, you are much better off to break silos by first trying to shift culture (see Step 8), and only after some progress has been made, change the organizational structure to accelerate change. A company's true structure is how it works in fact, not the boxes on a sheet of paper.

Expand measures of success for the organization.

If you don't measure the right success criteria, how can you possibly know how you are doing? Savvy organizations increasingly develop indicators tailored to their company for measuring whether or not business model and growth strategy is being executed and if it is indeed creating desired results. It is important that the indicator contain both leading and lagging measures of success.

The objectives of a broader set of measures than financial ones alone include the following:

- Provide a set of performance measures that capture the intent of the business model strategy and help drive it forward.
- Expand management's focus to include all of those capabilities required to achieve the strategy.
- Direct the focus of the entire organization toward those performance measures critical to achieving the strategic goals of the organization.
- Create a dynamic performance measurement system that adapts to the changing needs of the business.
- Provide a basis for setting long-term performance objectives that drive performance improvements.

Let go of business.

Every business faces a moment of truth with its new business model when it must turn away business to dramatically increase focus on its new direction. For example, the company may, in defining its desired business model, decide to focus on one market, not the three currently served. Trying to succeed in multiple markets or categories with contrasting requirements often leads to mediocre results, at best, in both markets or categories unless different free-standing business units can be created and there is some synergy among the units.

The execution challenge in this case is accepting one market as far more strategic than another. This requires no longer allocating resources and making changes in the company to succeed in three markets. The commercial sewing company discussed in Step 4 decided it needed to exit the medical market if it was to ever succeed with its new business model focused on marine companies. Exiting the medical market in a way that preserved the company's reputation became an important goal.

Similarly, when an architectural firm decided to target clients who understand and appreciate the power of contextual design and its interplay with function, it carefully delineated the characteristics of those target clients within the target market, segmented by type of facility. Although the firm was open to potential clients who may not understand this, it knew the market did segment into those who care significantly about aesthetic and working environment and those who care far less. As the partners committed to the new business model, the firm realized that a number of its current clients did not match the criteria. It committed over the next year to proactively finding new clients whose work would replace these clients. For some, the firm realized it had not dialogued high enough in the client organization to determine whether the firm met the criteria.

Sometimes, you can continue to be in all markets by recognizing that a non-strategic market is just that. Although Finfrock D-M-C now primarily serves as a full-service design-build construction firm, it still accepts straight precast concrete work from general contractors *if* it has excess capacity.

If you want to hang onto work that is no longer your primary focus, do so only if you can perform that work in the context of current capabilities. In any case, stop investing new resources to improve the no longer needed capabilities or to chase work that precludes obtaining work from strategic customers. Sometimes, because of customer demands, you must work with current customers to depart from a market. Other times, you may be able to sell part of your business to a company for whom that market is strategic. The same argument can apply to departing from a product category, not just a market.

ONE MORE TOOL—CULTURE CHANGE

The final tool leadership teams use to achieve strategic goals is culture change—a change in the norms and beliefs and values that drive people to work the way they work, individually and as teams. We turn to this powerful tool in Step 8.

Recognizing That Change Happens Here

Before this step, the work you did was all thought and no action. With Step 7 the rubber meets the road, and people will be called on to actually change how they do their work—and often how they *think* about their work. This is where change becomes real, which is why it's also where you will encounter previously hidden resistance. The largest resistance will come as a refusal to reallocate resources from the old business model to the new business model. Fear of changing the old business model, and therefore over-funding it, will starve the new business model.

To overcome this resistance to change, you must keep your business's aspiration front and center in all communications. And you must find small early victories that demonstrate the advantages of change. Communicating these victories is a vital role of leadership. Publicly honor coworkers whose efforts are consistent with the corporate aspiration and new business model.

Another tactic is to remind people of the risks of the status quo—which are often far greater than the risks of change. You will not gain new business if you are not willing to give up some other business that is inconsistent with where you want to head. Shifting people's roles can help break down resistance to change—if placed in new roles, managers have less tendency to hold onto the old business.

BUILD ON THE MOMENTS OF TRUTH

Look out for moments of truth—decisions and behaviors the leadership must make in which it either demonstrates its commitment to the new model or shows by action that change isn't really going to happen or happen quickly. Face your moment of truth and allocate resources to the new business model and make other hard decisions consistent with it and your aspirations. Success will follow. You'll rarely regret decisions made to secure a far better business. You will regret never trying.

In addition to creating an annual plan that aligns with the new business model and strategic goals, the leadership team must manage to that plan. It must ensure that important milestones are met and that the change that is desired starts to come into play. If plans sit on a shelf, you will be in the same commodity market muck one year from today. Here are some questions you can ask going forward to make sure your company fully integrates its new business model:

- Is our competitive strategy known and understood across the organization?

- Do we understand which processes are or will be at the heart of our marketplace and financial success?

- Do individuals, departments, and process teams know how they contribute to our points of differentiation and core competencies?

- Do we have the right skills? Are we creating, preserving, and enhancing our core competencies?

- Are we structured effectively to execute our strategies?

- In our estimation, can one person serve as both the marketing and the sales professional (i.e., can a marketing professional cover sales and vice versa)?

- What is not getting done in our organization when sales is responsible for both the sales and the marketing roles?

- Does our company have a market-understanding process in place that is as strong as or stronger than its financial/operational information process?

- Are our decisions and actions integrated around a well-conceived, long-term business model strategy? Who in our organization is helping us define the strategy and ensure that it "works" in the marketplace?

- Are our measures consistent with our strategies? Do we have both leading and lagging indicators of success in strategy execution?

- Are our planning systems focusing everyone in the same direction? Is it the right direction?

- Are we deploying process improvement resources on the highest payback and most strategic processes?

- Are we "fixing" processes when we should be redesigning them from scratch?

- How should we change our budget process to better support our desire to be strategic leaders and to ensure that we are competing as a differentiated company rather than a company facing growing commodity competition?

Conclusion

Many companies have great planning systems, but they are focused on financial outcomes alone. Others have great ideas about how to be different from the competition, but their ideas never get translated into actions. Year by year, both types of organizations are doing the same old things. In both cases, companies fail their people and their customers. In other words,

- Companies need to get different *and* get better.
- Companies competing as commodities need new strategies.
- Existing market leaders need enhanced points of differentiation and stronger barriers to copycat competition.
- All companies must develop even better execution skills to create the organization's desired future.

Alignment is the part of the change process where the rubber meets the road. Alignment is achieved through a balanced new-products portfolio, marketing and sales planning, operations planning, financial planning, and an accurate yardstick for measuring performance and incentives that encourage stronger performance.

The planning frameworks outlined in this chapter serve to align the work of the organization with its strategies to actually change (versus *plan* to change) the organization. But they serve other roles, as well. This framework places leadership in the role of creating processes to deploy resources and align activities, thereby pulling leaders out of the work of daily operations. This opens the space for others to do the daily work, thereby enabling all employees to develop and use their inherent gifts. Use of this framework also creates a feeling of community: We are all in this together, each with distinct and important roles. Aligned planning is also a key tool for building collaboration and tackling the systemic causes of distrust and weakened relationships across parts of the organization. With all these advantages, what are you waiting for?

Changes in the work and how people work together improve in the presence of strong leadership. A strategic leader always uses today's work to model desired behavior, to foster change and renewal, to maintain spirit and momentum, to help others know and fully use their gifts, and to reinforce an inspiring and meaningful business aspiration. When leaders do this work, the vision becomes reality, and the company or business unit's deeper purpose is fulfilled.

STEP 7 KEY POINTS

Establish strategic goals and create an annual planning process to achieve them.

Desired goals:

- ✔ Define three-year strategic goals.
- ✔ Define the organization's annual business plan to achieve the strategic goals. The business plan contains six aligned parts: the marketing plan; the sales plan; the operations plan; the products or services plan; the corporate citizenship plan; and the financial plan.

Keys to success:

- ✔ Make sure your goals are specific, measurable, and accompanied by strategies to achieve them and action plans and timetables for moving forward.
- ✔ Encourage broad-based participation.
- ✔ Have concise, easy to measure, actionable goals and objectives.
- ✔ Ensure organizational and process focus before functional focus.
- ✔ Regularly check progress against the business plan and strategic goals, making adjustments and overcoming barriers to success as necessary.

Create differentiation in fact, not just on paper.

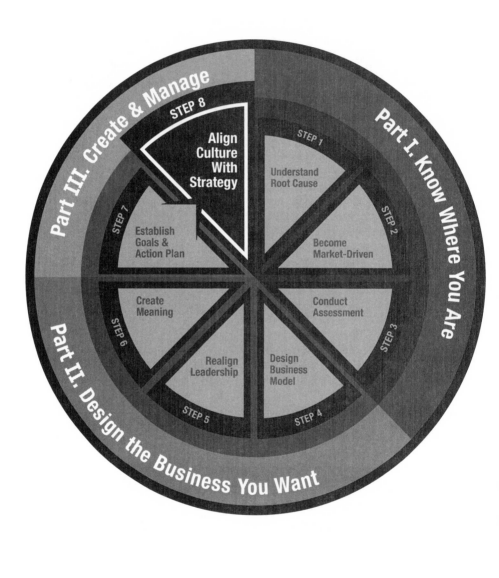

Step 8

Align Culture with Strategy

Whether culture is a catalyst or barrier to change depends upon the leadership team.[19]

John's direct reports were the leaders of four stand-alone profit centers or business units that manufactured consumer products. The arrangement worked well as it drove decision making to a lower level and allowed him to focus on acquisitions and other future-oriented activities. There was only one problem, but it was a huge one. Potential synergies across the four business units were not being realized. Although physical co-location was impossible because the company's products were dependent on local resources and therefore production needed to be near customers, John thought that sales, marketing, project management, and engineering could be highly leveraged across all four profit centers.

John decided to reorganize the company around four core processes: getting the order; designing the offering; making the offering; and shipping and installing the offering. (Finance and Human Resources were joined into a team called Support the Teams.) Leaders of the stand-alone units were placed in charge of one of the processes.

Little did John anticipate just how hard the change would be to achieve. Once in competition with each other, these four leaders now had to work collaboratively both to complete day-to-day work and to execute changes to improve how the work got done or to introduce additional offerings. The competitive relationship among these four leaders was mirrored at all levels of the organization. Were the need to capture synergies not so imperative from a financial and customer-delight perspective, John would never have advised a change in the company's structure and, it turned out, culture.

John's company had gotten where it was due to a locally cohesive but internally competitive culture. Now the culture needed to shift to one that was collaborative within and across locations. This would require employees at all levels of the organization to change how they worked together and to redefine success at an individual and team level. The change was hardest at the senior level, as there were many past events that had built a level of distrust among the leaders. When the company was organized as four units, the distrust could be ignored except during development of shared marketing communication tools. Now distrust became a front-and-center barrier to success.

John hired an organizational development leader to help the leaders talk through past issues that had given rise to the distrust. The team also spent considerable time discussing and understanding why having teams across locations work together was so imperative to the company's longer-term success. As the leaders learned and made changes, modeling collaboration in their actions, other employees followed. The road was bumpy to be sure, but over time the culture moved toward collaboration across all locations. The business return was significant. In addition to capturing cost savings and improving supply chain performance and retail customer and consumer benefits, it was easier to recruit new engineering and sales talent as potential hires saw a larger set of opportunities in the company for their career.

As John discovered, the culture of an organization determines the predominant way that people do their work and interact with each other. A culture can be like the flow of a river. Fish are not aware they are in a river—but their movements are affected by the flow. The flow can also make a canoe trip pleasant or painfully slow, or keep the canoe locked in an eddy from which the paddlers cannot escape. Or, as a friend commented, "Culture eats strategy for breakfast."

Many companies who have attempted to break out of commodity competition by defining a new business model have gotten stuck when it came to implementation because, like John's company, their cultures worked in opposition to the required changes. Fortunately, unlike a river's flow, you *can* change corporate culture. It may be the hardest part of your job because it requires personal change.

YOU ARE HERE

Link to previous steps: The corporate aspiration and proposed new business model open leaders' minds to new possibilities. Action planning from Step 7 creates a road map for change that builds needed confidence. This step, our last, broadens the view of the future in ways that create personal changes in leaders, personal changes that are catalysts for organizational change.

Expected outcome: Identification of one or two shifts in the company's culture will unlock the full power of the strategically differentiated business model. The leadership and management team members will look and sound different when working with one another and communicating to the rest of the organization.

Who is involved: The leadership team must in its work with members model how the team wants individuals to work together within the organization. Therefore culture change starts in the leadership team and with personal change in leaders. Over time, the work in this step is brought into a still larger management team.

Why this step is important: Organizations rarely change in significant ways if people do not change. Identifying the personal changes needed to become a stronger and more successful company and a more effective leadership team is at the heart of corporate change.

The culture within an organization is formed by and reflects the basic assumptions and beliefs that are shared by members of the organization. These assumptions and beliefs operate unconsciously, and they define the organization's view of

CORPORATE CULTURE

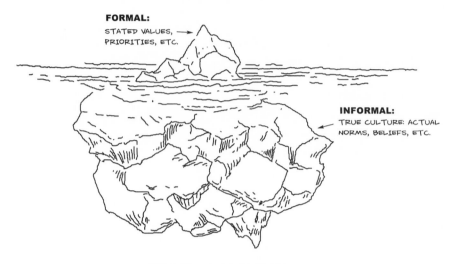

**CULTURE IS LIKE AN ICEBERG.
THE TRUE CULTURE IS HIDDEN BELOW THE WATER LINE.**

itself and its environment. Culture is to an organization what air is to humans—everywhere, but not necessarily visible to the eye or conscious to the mind.

When a company lives by its guiding principles, there is strong alignment between the stated values of the organization and its culture. Where guiding principles are words only, the underlying norms of behavior for the firm are far more descriptive of the organization's culture. Therefore, you can think about the culture as an iceberg. There are the formal, or overt, aspects, which is the way we *say* work gets done. Stated values, structures, systems, and other formal items fall above the water line. Then there are the informal, or covert, aspects, which determine the way work *really* gets done. Beliefs, assumptions, emotions, attitudes about the formal items, and patterned ways of interacting—group norms—are below the water line, driving how the company works in fact.

In this step, we'll talk about the importance of being open to personal change, how to tell whether your corporate culture is compatible or incompatible with your new business model, and how to successfully address culture change.

Enabling versus Disabling Cultures

There are no good or bad cultures when it comes to achieving major change, only *enabling* or *disabling* cultural attributes, given your organization's business model, purpose, guiding principles, and vision.

- An enabling attribute is an attitude, belief, or way of working that is consistent with the new strategically differentiated business model. For example, if your goal is to provide better end-to-end experience for your customers, an enabling attribute would be the willingness for people to collaborate across functions.

- A disabling attribute is one that stands in the way of change—or even works against the desired change. For example, a culture in which people worked in functional silos without regard for other parts of the organization would work against the ability to provide better end-to-end customer experiences.

LOOK FOR UNDISCUSSABLES

If the disabling elements in your culture outweigh the enabling elements, you will find a lot of "undiscussables" in the organization—issues people talk about with spouses and close work associates, but not with people involved in the issue or who could solve the issue. People will refrain from speaking up about the undiscussable even if they see something happen that they know is counterproductive. These undiscussables undermine the ability of the organization to achieve its vision.

The trouble leaders run into is that something that was once an enabling norm can turn into a disabling norm under a new business model and set of strategic goals. For example, a company that was financially driven, trying to win the low-cost game, would want very little risk taking. This would become a disabling norm if a new value proposition required significant new product innovation. The company would need a new cultural attribute of measured risk taking to succeed in creating new product solutions.

Examples of disabling cultural norms and beliefs include the following:

- Employees outwardly agree with leadership, even if they disagree. Think about a failed initiative in your organization whose failure was more costly than it had to be because of this norm.

- There is much debate before a decision is made, with each group presenting its strongest case, when no side is open to hearing or understanding what the other side is explaining.

- No risk is worth taking.

- Do whatever the boss says, period.

Exposing disabling norms is hard work—in part because of the negative impact of the norm itself. People are not about to say that they've learned not to speak their minds. *The only way through this quagmire is to start with individual change*. Once people see that the company leaders are acting differently, they will be more willing to change themselves.

Recognizing That Culture Change Starts with Individual Change

"It is striking to me that so many new programs that initiate change in organizations fail. It is also striking that once a change effort fails, the effort tends to be ignored. These failures are seldom analyzed. Such analysis would be too painful. As a result, little learning takes place.

When we experience failure, it is natural to externalize the problem—to blame some factor that was outside our control. Once in a while that actually does happen. But I have seldom heard anyone say, "The change didn't happen because I failed to model the change process for everyone. I failed to reinvent myself. It was a failure of courage on my part."

—Robert Quinn, writing in *Deep Change*[20]

The culture of an organization describes the interpersonal relationships between individuals that affect how they work with one another. Culture change doesn't happen without individuals and their interpersonal relationships changing. That means personal change is a necessary condition for cultural change. As a result, the process of planning and implementing change is not just an adaptation of the organization to the market changes or a new vision of success or a new business model but a deeper, personal, under-the-skin type of adaptation and change as well.

When change efforts focus only on organizational changes (objectives, skills, structure), you're likely to see impatience and resistance start to rise. Many leaders have learned hard lessons by watching habitual ways of getting things done crowd out momentum for change. Excuses include "The middle managers didn't buy in," "The CEO never demonstrated personal support," and "The employees never really got on board."

In fact, most change efforts fail as Quinn notes because the leaders themselves failed to change, not because the organization failed to choose a great strategy. They fail to make the personal changes needed to truly unleash the potential of their organization and its new business model.

LINK PERSONAL CHANGE TO ORGANIZATIONAL RESULTS

Change at the enterprise level is objective and result oriented. It moves forward in a linear fashion. Personal change is emotional and moves forward by discovery in an organic, often unplanned way. The tensions and connections between these two change processes are often the least conscious and most ignored part of organizational dynamics. Yet, it is exactly the connection between the enterprise side and interpersonal side that is the most important part of the change process and the place where change initiatives get "stuck." What natural leaders implicitly do is unite both of these sides. We believe this unification can be learned.

The types of personal changes we're talking about are the types that are visible to others inside and outside the firm. For example—a CEO speaking more openly and candidly, a VP listening to his peer before saying what he thinks is the right answer, and being influenced by the other VPs' insights. Creating these changes involves challenging our personal beliefs, assumptions, and goals. It includes owning how we genuinely react at a visceral level to the changes going on in the organization. It also involves owning how our current working patterns and relationships are creating the exact situations that we want to see changed.

Interpersonal key: Beliefs drive perception, which then drives reality.

Stu is an interior designer in an architectural firm who has a very messy desk. He is often rushing around, barely getting things done on time. If you encountered Stu as his new boss, would you be more likely to think . . .

- Stu is entrusted with a lot of duties.
- Stu is very inefficient.
- Stu has too much to do.
- Stu is a control freak and won't let anyone help him.
- People don't like Stu and won't offer to help him.

The answer, of course, is that we can't tell from observations of Stu's desk what's going on with Stu. The fact of the matter is that our beliefs and values determine our behavior toward others. For example, if we value relationships and believe associates have good intentions, our approach as leaders will differ from when we do not value relationships and distrust the motivations of peers.[21] Positive beliefs about people will lead a new boss to assume that Stu is entrusted with a lot of duties.

Personal change is hard because it requires a revision of old assumptions or beliefs, such as negative beliefs about others (e.g., management, employees, the union, the finance department). These assumptions are often deeply colored by our individual architecture of the past: how we were shaped by family values and dynamics, our views of peers and friends, educational experiences, the culture of our professional discipline, and specific past work experiences. The beliefs are often invisible, like the atmosphere. And, in turn, they have led to a particular formula for behavior that we recognize as our comfort zone. The interweaving of beliefs, assumptions, and behaviors may be dysfunctional (out of alignment with what is needed in the organization), but it feels like a rational approach to the way the world is as seen from our individual perspective.

Yet our beliefs affect the reality that emerges. If, as Stu's new boss, you immediately conclude that Stu is inefficient, you risk relating to Stu in a way that will worsen his performance and drive him out of the organization. If you think he is highly valued and relate to him as such, his performance is likely to improve. *To change reality, we must change our beliefs and values.* This is why organizational change must be accomplished by starting with change at the personal level.

(Later in this chapter we'll discuss how to create a shared personal development environment that expedites and best supports personal change among leaders in your organization.)

Trust plays an important role in personal change.

A key factor that makes personal change difficult is fear. No one can make another person face personal fears. This can be done only voluntarily. Overcoming fear requires a certain amount of self-trust. For example, exploring performance issues or patterns of behavior that stand in the way of individual or organizational success can be very tough, particularly for anyone with a deep investment in concealing his or her human flaws.

The lesson is that personal change requires safety and motivation. The desire for change is created when there is a personal reward from change. In contrast, threats for *not* changing create, at best, compliance. This is why cultural change efforts fail unless there is a motivation to change, which can come only with a shared, meaningful vision of the organization, a purpose that goes well beyond making money for the owners and higher bonuses for senior leaders, and a deeper understanding of market forces.

Motivation is necessary but not sufficient for personal change to occur. The second key is trust—trust in one's self and in others. Without that, people hunker into defensive positions, and their efforts to create change fall victim to forces that work to maintain the status quo. Trust erodes when emotionally distant change models, processes, and methods are used (i.e., when leaders steer clear of the emotional context that underlies the formal change initiative). This emotional context is another iceberg—only the tip is seen at the water's surface. When change activities become acting *on* an organization or group of people, rather than acting *with* it, when change activities focus only on the tip of the iceberg and not the totality, change momentum stops.

Overcoming fear and building trust are more difficult than gaining motivation. Overcoming fear requires trusting ourselves to explore how our actions inhibit the creation of the desired working relationships, and trusting others to provide feedback related to this. Trust building takes time and attention. Leaders start to build trust by asking for feedback and listening so as to be influenced by others.

GO BEYOND BUY-IN

The benefits of trust in the context of personal changes and changes in working relationships include:

- Telling the truth to oneself and then to one another
- Believing that others are telling the truth
- Collaborating to find solutions when the work does not correspond to what is desired
- Effectively asking for and providing feedback to others so as to learn how an individual is helping or hindering the change initiative
- Improving and changing systems without becoming mired in negative assumptions about others' motives, skills, or agendas
- Surfacing "undiscussables" (i.e., items discussed with others, but not the people involved and other people who could directly do something about the issue) before they become a barrier to change. Don't try to actually discuss the undiscussables at the meeting where you identify them. Rather, set up a separate meeting in which people address these issues directly.
- Using conflicts constructively to build understanding and learning

Trust cannot develop when there is no shared, understood, and accepted aspiration or strategy for the organization. Unintentionally, people assign adverse motives when a lack of alignment on what the strategy is leads to individuals acting on different agendas. Thus, we come full circle in understanding the relationship between the enterprise change agenda and the changes in working relationships—that is, culture—required to enable and fully realize the full potential of enterprise-side changes.

Leading the Change: Creating a Shared Personal Development Environment

Unfortunately, building trust is often excluded from the leadership team's agenda when, in fact, it is the development of trust within the leadership team that models what needs to happen for trust and personal change to develop elsewhere in the organization. If the head of manufacturing and the head of engineering do not trust one another, it is unlikely that engineering and manufacturing personnel will work together in ways that ensure the overall success of new systems and new strategies. Thus, models of organizational change must incorporate activities that increase the level of personal and interpersonal trust in the organization—starting with the leadership team.

WHY LEADERS KEEP DISCUSSION OF PERSONAL CHANGE AND TRUST BUILDING OUT OF THE EXECUTIVE SUITE

- There is a belief that business and personal life do not go together.

- There is a fear of being vulnerable in this discussion—of people taking advantage of you—a fear of opening Pandora's box.

- Many managers do not see all the connections between their personal behavior and business results, or they fail to see how their deeply held beliefs, values, and assumptions impact their behavior.

- People do not want to hear negative feedback about their interpersonal relationship skills.

- No permission, time, or validation is given to these topics. As such, they do not show up on anyone's agenda, except in private discussions of close friends at work.

- To introduce discussion of trust and personal change in an organization is to shift the focus from head to heart, and from hierarchy to community. Many leaders feel threatened by this loss of control, especially when their mental model of leadership's role in business success is to be smarter than other people and therefore ensure that better decisions are made.

How can you build trust within the leadership team and encourage all leaders to undergo personal changes that support the desired culture change?

The best approach is to create a *shared personal development initiative* to bring traditional career and leadership/management development discussions into a group setting. (One-on-ones can still exist, but commitments made here and insights gained here should be shared within the team if they advance the team's effectiveness and trust levels.) The use of a shared personal development effort enhances individuals' motivation to change because it helps make it clear that the changes asked of people are linked to the business model, business plan, and aspiration. If people own these decisions, they will own personal change. This explains why active involvement of all leaders and others in setting new directions is so vital. Top-down change efforts with no bottom-up involvement and voice do not work.

The aim of a personal development initiative is to help leaders identify the one or two personal changes they must each make to be in alignment with the desired direction of the organization so that leaders' efforts add to—rather than inhibit—the success of the organization in achieving its aspiration. Clearly, economic literacy, an understanding of strategy, and alignment of team and individual objectives with the organization's change initiative are critical. What we are talking about here is additional. It is how the individual must change his or her own personal behaviors and relationships with others to further drive the change initiative. Although this topic is discussed in performance reviews, it is rarely revealed to others. Yet, discussing individual gaps and gifts of leaders as a group helps them better understand and support one another's and the team's development as leaders.

The shared nature of the personal development initiative is critical to unlocking interpersonal relationship patterns, which are at the heart of the existing culture. It is only when individuals reveal the "real stuff" in personal development that the illusions one person has about another person get shattered and a new set of beliefs and assumptions can develop that foster deeper trust.

What would this initiative look like for the leadership team, where the shared personal development environment and personal growth must start? It would include activities such as these:

- Understanding the goal of the team and writing its charter (see Step 5)

- Identifying individual leaders' strengths and weaknesses

- Identifying how things work today in the leadership team under the old culture and what it would look like if desired culture change occurred

- Identifying undiscussables and having ongoing deliberations of these issues in a way that leads to their resolution

- Discussing where the organization is out of alignment in trying to achieve its vision and how the leadership team's behaviors are contributing to the misalignment

- Conducting training sessions on listening, speaking up, and driving fear out of the workplace

- Examining case studies of how other leaders and leadership team members have changed personally

- Creating internal learning conferences tailored to company-specific business issues

- Holding meetings between the leadership team and other teams to gather feedback on how they are helping and/or hindering the organization's change process

- Gathering feedback from others in the organization related to progress on key dimensions of organizational changes, including culture change

- Facilitating team problem solving in ways that reinforce the culture the leadership team is trying to create

- Surfacing the beliefs and assumptions that give rise to how a person relates to others, and using open dialogue between individuals with difficult interpersonal relationships to break through these beliefs and assumptions

How the personal development initiative is created and run is critical to its success. What doesn't work is for leaders, acting alone or with their boss, to decide what types of changes are needed in their behavior. Rather, there needs to be a shared process that is linked to desired changes in the business. This linkage will increase the chances that the behavioral changes will drive the desired strategic changes, improve motivation for interpersonal change, and build a deeper sense of community within the organization.

Using Three Ingredients of Culture Change

The three ingredients for creating successful culture change are *where*, *what*, and *how*.

Where should culture change start?

Where you begin with culture change depends on the levels of trust and openness within the organization. If there is a lack of openness within the leadership team or between the team and the rest of the organization, the culture change must start strictly at the top and then open up to others. If the leadership team is working well—that is, there's a high level of trust and openness within the group—then this conversation can occur with a broader array of managers and coworkers. If there is a strong set of issues between two or more members of the leadership team, resolving those issues first is necessary.

What should culture change embrace?

The following are some standard elements of a culture that encourage sustained differentiation and ease execution of a new or modified business model:

- Working collaboratively (first discussed in Step 5) is vitally important. This does not mean that individual initiatives are no longer important. Competition for the top slots will still exist. The intent is that people work together to advance the well-being of the company when there are important interdependencies between different parts of the organization. Key enabling norms for collaboration are as follows:
  - Work from the premise that no one person has the whole answer.

- Seek common ground.
- Use conflicts constructively to learn and to find win-win answers.
- Freeze negative assumptions about other's motives.
- Ask for and provide feedback in order to consciously build trust.
- Speak the truth versus feigning politeness.

- Be open to change.

- Make decisions with data, not anecdotes, whenever you can. Present the facts and the true case, not your version of the facts and the spin that hides the issues.

- Delegate, whenever someone else can do the work, so that you can focus on work that only you can do. This fosters growth of your staff and advances the overall capacity of the organization.

- Broaden the boundaries of your work so that more time is spent with customers and you are more flexible with coworkers about what work gets done in what parts of the organization.

BUILD ON WHERE YOU ARE; PICK CHANGES IMPORTANT TO *YOUR* BUSINESS

Ideally, your company already has some of these change-enabling behaviors built into its culture. If so, emphasize those strengths as you move forward. If you're lacking in many areas, don't get overwhelmed. You don't need all of them in order to move forward and become strategically differentiated. Rather, identify which of these norms would most help your company and focus on those areas.

Above all, don't try to do too much at one time. Our own experience is that culture changes slowly, and it is the hardest thing in a company to change. Focus on one shift at a time, and then the change will be easier and more successful. Work with the positive elements of the culture at all times to effect change, because people asked to change are less threatened when many things stay the same.

There will be some changes that are specific to your business model. Let's turn to that conversation now.

How can you identify and bring about desired culture change?

Although culture change does not follow a sequential, linear path, leadership teams can follow a basic framework to move culture change forward.

- *Define the current culture: identify the gap between reality and desire.* Ask new employees, close business partners, and a broad array of employees about their observations of the implicit norms and beliefs in the company. If necessary, you may want to hire an outside human resource or organizational development consulting firm to do a formal study. Review the Step 6 work from the company-wide effort to define the organization's aspiration, including a discussion of strategies derived from the new business model. Clues to culture change exist in feedback gathered at this company meeting.

- *Determine barriers to change.* Ask, "What barriers to executing our new strategy will arise from *how we do our work* and *how we work together?* What barriers in our culture will we encounter in trying to execute these strategies?" Your goal is to get to the heart of cultural norms that will prevent or weaken successful execution of new strategic directions and key initiatives.

- *Discuss the strengths of the current culture and the ways people relate to one another.* Ask, "What's going right, in terms of our relationships, that we will always want to hold onto because they serve as a strong foundation for our success and are needed for successful execution of the new business model?" Be sure to talk about the implicit values that people genuinely see at work in the organization.

DETERMINE WHAT'S WORKED, OR NOT, IN THE PAST

Think about a project, product, or client where you were working at your very best and delivering on your value proposition (or getting close to it). What were you doing that enabled that success?

Also look to your past to identify what has stood in the way of successful change. Ask, "When have we tried to deliver elements of our value proposition in the past? What got in the way?"

- *Discuss how to build on enabling norms and values (i.e., those that help meet the challenges posed by the strategic initiatives).* Ask: "What changes in these norms and values could we agree to that could reduce the barriers we discussed and increase the probability that our strategies will be executed successfully?"

- *Discuss and agree on a new way of relating to one another (one new norm of behavior) that will help leaders and employees make the types of changes needed to support the new business model.* Also reach agreement on how to work with one another when the new norm is not being followed. This may take time. Don't force compliance.

- *Develop a profile of how specific challenges can be addressed.* Think about specific types of challenges the company will face in executing its business model. Develop a profile of how each issue would be handled in the old way of working and how you'd like the issue to be addressed under the new way of working.

- *Identify personal development work for company leaders.* Consider both work they should do alone plus any shared development that leaders will do as a team.

- *Identify and address undiscussables that need to be exposed.* Look for underlying issues the organization has failed to address in the past that have led to interpersonal tensions between groups or individuals within the organization. Decide how to more openly address those undiscussables.

CULTURE CHANGE IN ACTION

When Robert Finfrock did this work during the conversion of his company from a precast concrete manufacturer to a full-service design-manufacture-construct firm, the management team discovered that its decades-long commitment to integrity, quality, and cost-effectiveness would not be enough to unlock the full potential of a new business model.

Robert has personally shifted his thinking from overseeing day-to-day operations to long-range thinking. It took time, but he built a great team around him to manage the day-to-day. He spends his time asking and answering, "What do we need to be doing differently today to ensure our success tomorrow?"

Key elements of Finfrock D-M-C's new culture, which evolved over time, include the following:

- *Pay more attention to learning, more attention to challenging how you do things, and more openness to change.* Becoming more curious as individuals is a key driver of this.

- *Focus on using measurement and objectivity.* The company uses objective tools to make the best decisions rather than position power and debating skills.

- *Pay attention to details that engineers might otherwise dismiss.* This has driven Robert's firm to get better and better in the aesthetic and the functional performance of the completed structures his company designs, manufactures, and constructs.

Conclusion

Culture change is not something you impose on others. It is something you step into yourself as a leader. Therefore, culture change is about the hardest but most important work of the leadership team. We know this intuitively, but often, work on culture change is stopped by seemingly more urgent needs. In fact, it is our fear of stepping into the personal dimensions of culture change and our fear that we lack talent to lead culture change that often stop culture change efforts, and therefore business transformation, dead in their tracks. Give yourself permission to fail, as that opens the door for others to try. Without risk taking, there can be no personal change or culture change.

STEP 8 KEY POINTS

Align culture with strategy by initiating personal change that enhances the probability of successful execution of the new business model strategy.

Desired goals:

✔ Identify one shift in how leaders will work together that will unlock the full power of the differentiated business model. This shift must start in the leadership team.

Keys to success:

✔ Open your hearts and minds to the rest of the company.

✔ Be open to personal change.

✔ Listen—to self and to others.

✔ Have a realistic view of your organization's current culture—versus focusing exclusively on the culture you hope to create.

✔ Be patient. Accept that culture change takes time.

✔ Use existing elements of the culture to create change.

Whether culture is a catalyst or barrier to change depends upon the leadership team.

Epilogue

Pay attention to the ten commandments for staying out of commodity market quicksand.

The law of nemesis states that people copy a good thing. Branded-goods companies face this every day when Walgreens or Wal-Mart or a grocery store wholesaler introduces "me-too" lower-priced store-brand offerings. Therefore, an essential part of staying out of commodity-market muck is recycling through the eight-step framework. In early cycles, you will be tweaking your business model. But at some point, you will need a redefinition of the business model.

We have found that the following ten commandments help leaders maintain the discipline to keep their company out of commodity-market quicksand:

1. You must change the rules for how your market works, because if you don't, a smarter competitor will.

2. Never forget that all purchase decisions are based on perceived value. Being differentiated in ways that offer customers benefits and reduce their indirect costs increases your perceived value.

3. Build your market understanding process into a strategic advantage.

4. Build a core competency that is hard to replicate or a market position that is hard for others to enter. Being first into a new category and succeeding from the start is a good indicator that you have accomplished just this.

5. Focus on the real competition—the marketplace—not your peers.

6. Honor your strategic customers and build your company around them. Not all customers or market segments are strategic.

7. Never conduct your strategic assessment at the start of budget cycle.

8. Invest in your personal growth as a leader and as a leadership team. The capacity of your company to change will depend on it.

9. Live your purpose, vision, and guiding principles. They determine whether people show up every day with passion or in pursuit of a paycheck.

10. Keep improving your value proposition and aligning everything to it. At the same time, be ready to create an entirely different business model before the current one is copied by your competition.

We wish you all our best as you move into the most important task of leadership—creating a thriving business that enables colleagues and the company itself to achieve more of their full potential.

Notes

1. W. C. Kim and R. Maubourgne, *Blue Ocean Strategy* (Boston: Harvard Business School Press, 2005).

2. M. Lele, *Monopoly Rules* (New York: Crown Business, 2005).

3. J. Calloway, *Becoming a Category of One* (Hoboken, NJ: John Wiley & Sons, 2003).

4. Clayton Christensen has written extensively on innovation. See C. Christensen and M. Raynor, *The Innovator's Solution: Creating and Sustaining Successful Growth* (Boston: Harvard Business School Press, 2003).

5. The company used a different name initially, which was then changed to its current name, Finfrock Design-Manufacture-Construct, Inc.

6. Much of the core competency material reflects the excellent work of C. K. Prahalad and Gary Hamel in C. K. Prahalad and G. Hamel, *Competing for the Future* (Boston: Harvard Business School Press, 1996). More recently, C. Zook expanded on the application of core competencies in C. Zook, *Unstoppable* (Boston: Harvard Business School Press, 2007).

7. C. K. Prahalad and G. Hamel, "The Core Competencies of the Corporation," *Harvard Business Review On Point* (2003): 15.

8. J. Collins, *Good to Great* (New York: HarperCollins Publishers, 2001), 95.

9. In consumer goods businesses, consumer coupons or retailer incentives are other forms of price discounting.

10. P. Strebel, *Breakpoints* (Boston: Harvard Business School Press, 1992).

11. C. Argyris, *Reasons and Rationalizations: The Limits to Organizational Knowledge* (New York: Oxford University Press, 2004), 40.

12. R. Quinn, *Deep Change* (Hoboken, NJ: Jossey-Bass, 1996), 60.

13. Collins, ibid., 13.

14. From company public communications documents or how we, the authors, would state their deeper purpose upon reading these documents.

15. From Mary Kay's consulting clients.

16. From well-known case studies or Mary Kay's consulting clients.

17. A. Webber, "Destiny and the Job of the Leader," *Fast Company*, issue 3 (June/July 1996).

18. Max Depree, *Leadership Jazz* (New York: Dell Publishing, 1992), 89.

19. This chapter reflects Mary Kay's deep learning with Dan Oestreich, a Seattle-based organizational development consultant. Dan's work can be found in K. Ryan and D. Oestreich, *Driving Fear Out of the Workplace* (Hoboken, NJ: Jossey-Bass, 1998), and at http://unfoldingleadership.com.

20. Quinn, ibid., 34.

21. For further information on this topic, see P. Senge et al., *The Fifth Discipline Fieldbook* (New York: Doubleday, 1994), 242–46. The book cites multiple books that gave rise to their writing on Mental Models.

Note that chapter stories stem from actual business transformations. Some changes were made to protect confidentiality when deemed appropriate by Mary Kay and her client.

Index